Story Central Plus

CLIL Book 1

macmillan education

Lorena Peimbert

Contents

Chapter 1

What Tree Is This?

Science

1 **Look at the pictures. What do you think the text is about?**

Evergreen and Deciduous Trees

Look at the tables, chairs, books, and pencils in your classroom. They all come from trees! Let's learn more about them!

There are two types of trees. They are **evergreen** trees and **deciduous** trees.

Evergreen Trees

Their **leaves** are always green.

They have **narrow** leaves.

They have leaves all through the year.

Deciduous Trees

They have **broad** leaves.

Their leaves **change color** in the fall from green to red, orange, or brown!

They lose their leaves in the fall or winter.

2 **Listen and read. What type of tree has leaves that are always green?**

Read and Learn

1 Look and write.

broad leaf   deciduous tree   ~~evergreen tree~~   narrow leaves

1 evergreen tree 2 .... 3 .... 4 ....

2 Read and check.

1 Their leaves change color.	evergreen trees ☐	deciduous trees ☐
2 They have leaves all through the year.	evergreen trees ☐	deciduous trees ☐
3 Their leaves are always green.	evergreen trees ☐	deciduous trees ☐
4 They lose their leaves.	evergreen trees ☐	deciduous trees ☐

3 Ask and answer with a friend.

What is your favorite tree?

My favorite tree is a mango tree.

Did You Know?
Trees help clean the air.

Time to Think

1 Read and complete.

~~evergreen~~ green narrow year

2 Read and draw the leaves.

This is a deciduous tree. It has broad green leaves.	In the fall, its leaves change color. Now they are red and orange.	In the winter it loses its leaves.

Project

Prepare and Create

1 Work together and follow the instructions.

1 Choose a tree. Is it evergreen or deciduous?

2 Draw and cut out the leaves.

3 Draw and color your tree. Paste the leaves.

4 Label your tree.

Showcase

2 Share your tree with the class.

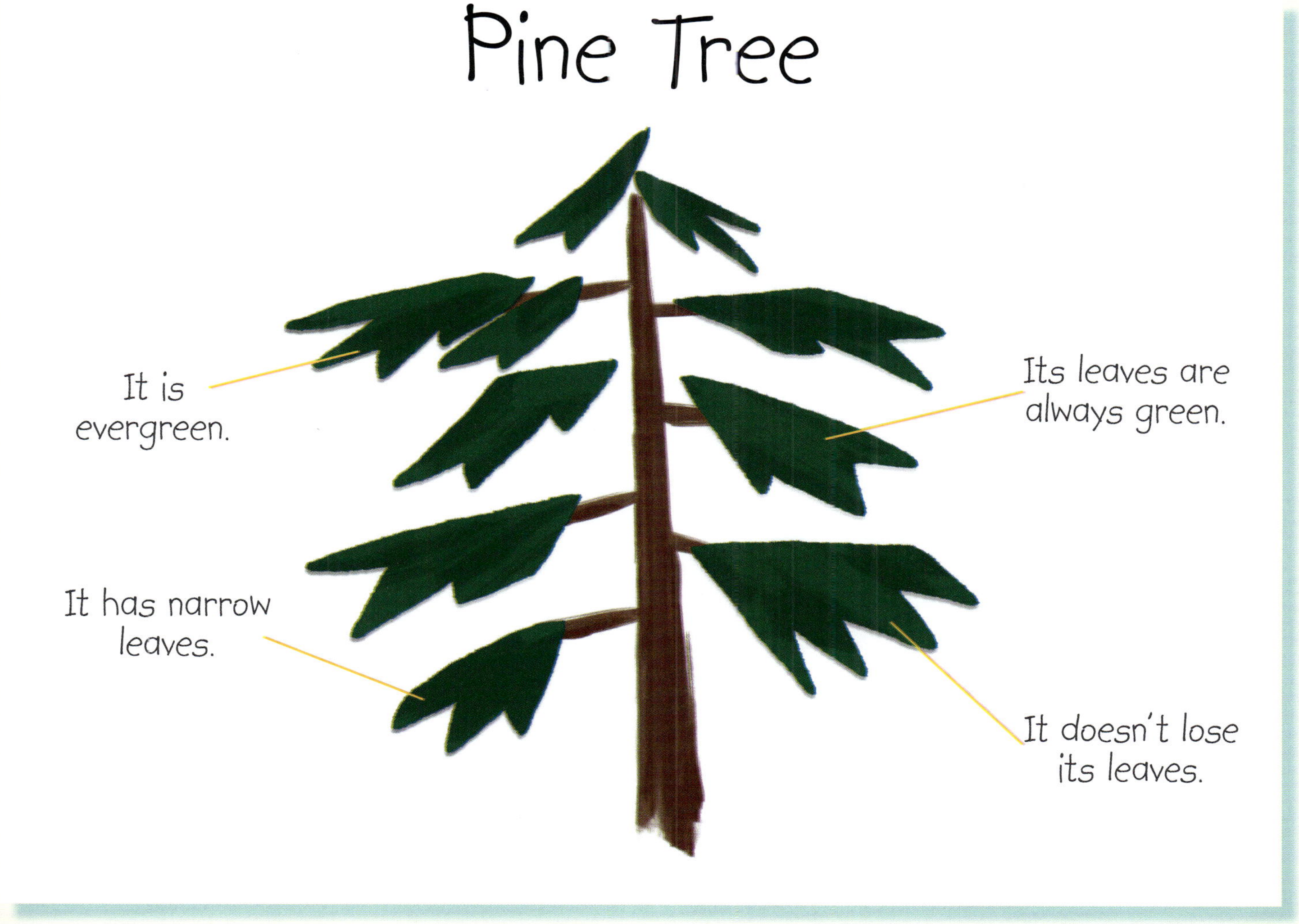

It's Our World

Why are trees imporant? Are there trees in your town?

Chapter 2

Shapes Are Fun!

Math

1 **Look at the title. What do you think the text is about?**

Do You Like to Play with 3D Shapes?

2D shapes are flat, like a square or a triangle. 3D shapes are fat, like a cube or a pyramid.

Toys are made of 3D shapes.

They are fun to play with. Let's look at them!

This is a ball.

A ball is a **sphere**!

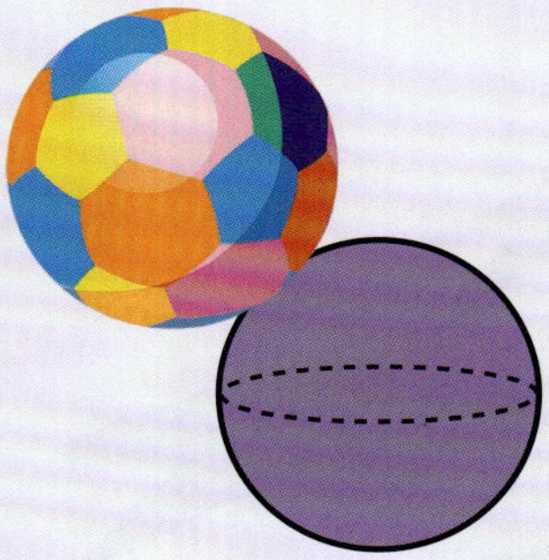

This is a robot.

Its head is a **cuboid**!

This is a box to put away your toys.

It's a **cube**!

This is a play tent.

It's a **pyramid**!

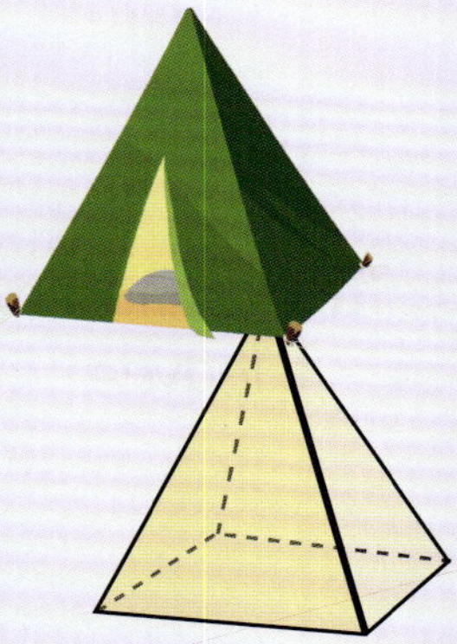

2 **Listen and read. What shape is a play tent?**

Did You Know?
Fruits have 3D shapes. An orange is a sphere.

Read and Learn

1 Find and write.

pyramidspherecubecuboid

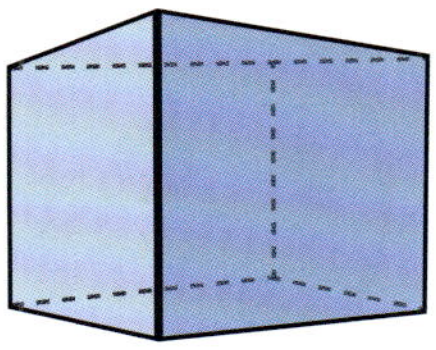
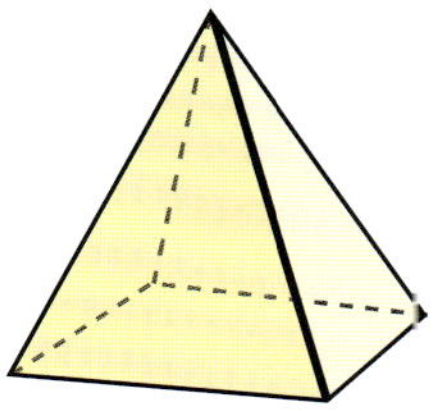
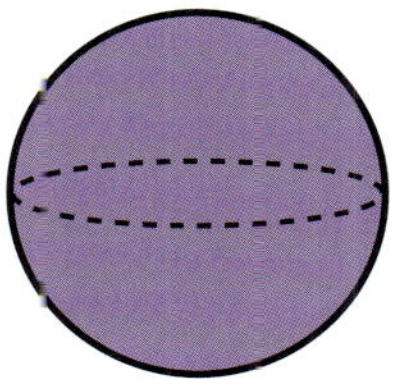
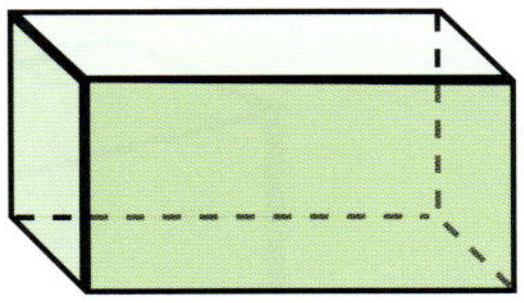

1 cube 2 ______ 3 ______ 4 ______

2 Choose and write. Then draw the toys.

ball box play tent ~~robot~~

1 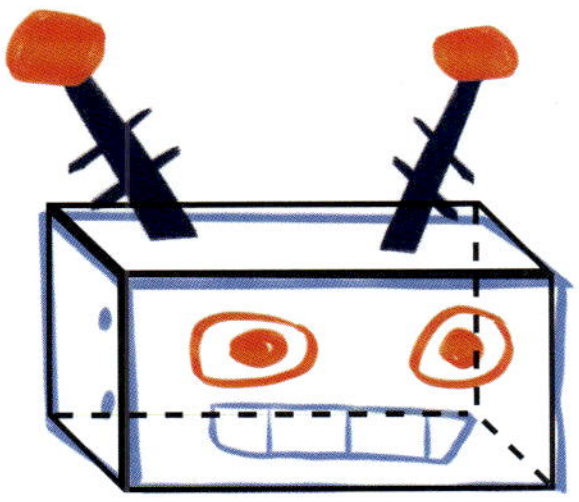
2 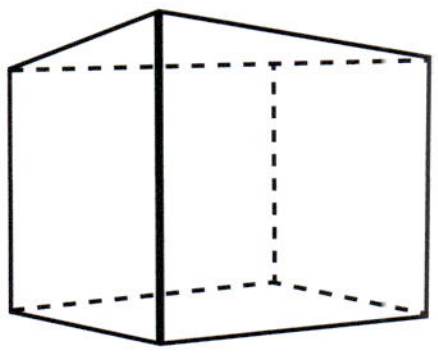
3 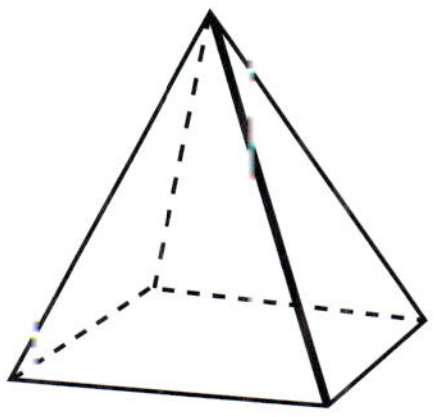
4 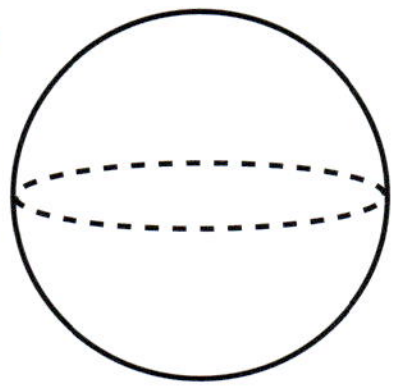

robot ______ ______ ______

3 Choose objects in your classroom with different 3D shapes. Then ask and answer with a friend.

What shape is this book?

It's a cuboid!

Time to Think

1 Find and match.

2 Color the shapes in Activity 1. Then complete.

Look! This is my car. It's made of 3D shapes! It has a
1 ....red cuboid.......... and a 2 .... !

This is my doll. Its body is a 3 .... !

This is my teddy bear. Its head is a 4 .... !

3 Choose one of your toys. Then complete.

My .... is made of 3D shapes!
(toy)

It has a ....
(color) (shape)

Project

Prepare and Create

1 Work together and follow the instructions.

1 Find or draw pictures of objects with different 3D shapes.

2 Cut out the pictures. Paste them on cards.

3 Put your cards face down on the table to play a memory game.

Showcase

2 Play a memory game. Find the cards with the same shape.

It's Our World

Do you share your toys with your friends?

Chapter 3

What Do They Eat?

Science

1 Look at the pictures. What do you think the text is about?

The Food Chain

the Sun

Plants and animals need food to live and grow, and it all starts with the Sun!

producer

Plants use light from the sun to make their food. They're **producers**. Animals eat food to get energy. They're **consumers**.

primary consumer

Primary consumers, like zebras and elephants, eat plants. Animals that eat plants are called **herbivores**.

secondary consumer

Secondary consumers, like lions and crocodiles, eat primary consumers. Animals that eat other animals are called **carnivores**.

Some animals, like birds and monkeys, are **omnivores**. They can be primary consumers (when they eat plants) and secondary consumers (when they eat other animals).

2 Listen and read. What do omnivores eat?

1 Look and circle.

1 herbivore / omnivore

2 carnivore / herbivore

3 omnivore / carnivore

4 herbivore / carnivore

2 Read and write T (True) or F (False).

1 Herbivores eat carnivores. ....

2 Animals can be producers. ....

3 Carnivores eat animals. ....

4 Omnivores eat plants and animals. ....

3 Ask and answer with a friend.

Did You Know?
Most animals eat different kinds of food, so they are part of different food chains.

Time to Think

1 **Complete the food chain with words from the box.**

primary consumer   producer   secondary consumer

the Sun	leaves	deer	tiger
	1	2	3 ....
		....	....

2 **Look and match.**

producer

primary consumer

secondary consumer

Project

Prepare and Create

1 Work together and follow the instructions.

1 Choose plants and animals to make a food chain mobile.

2 Cut out paper circles. Draw the Sun, the plants, and the animals you chose.

3 Make a hole at the top and bottom of each circle. Use string to tie the circles together and make your mobile.

Showcase

2 Share your food chain mobile with the class.

It's Our World

Do all people eat meat? Do you know any vegetarians?

Chapter 4

A Home Made of Snow

Social Sciences

1 **Look at the pictures. Are any of them similar to your home?**

What are homes made of?

This is a cabin. It's made of **wood**.
Do you think it has a yard?

This is a castle. It's made of **stone**.
Do you think it has a garage?

This is an igloo. It's made of **snow**.
Do you think it has a bathroom?

This is a house. It's made of **brick**.
Do you think it has a big bedroom?

2 **Listen and read. What kind of home is made of snow?**

1 Unscramble and write.

dowo ~~wons~~ cribk etons

1 snow 2 .... 3 .... 4 ....

2 Read and write T (True) or F (False).

1 A cabin is made of brick. ....
2 A castle is made of stone. ....
3 An igloo is made of snow. ....
4 A tent is made of wood. ....

3 Ask and answer with a friend.

What is your home made of?

It's made of wood!

Did You Know?
Windsor Castle is in the UK. It's made of stone.

Time to Think

1 Read and circle.

1 This floor is made of **wood** / **brick**.

2 This desk is made of **wood** / **stone**.

3 This chair is made of **stone** / **snow**.

4 This bed is made of **brick** / **stone**.

2 Read and complete.

1 My pencil is made of wood.

2 My ________ is made of ________.

3 My ________ is made of ________.

Project

Prepare and Create

1 Work together and follow the instructions.

1 Invent a house made of different materials.

2 Make a poster of your house.

Showcase

2 Share your house with the class.

It's Our World

What types of homes are in your country?

Chapter 5

How Do You Travel?

Geography

1 **Look at the title. What different types of vehicles can you name?**

Different Types of Vehicles

People use vehicles every day to go to different places. Here are three types of vehicles.

Human-powered vehicles

We move these vehicles with our arms and legs. Look at this **canoe**. It lets us travel on water, and do some exercise at the same time!

Animal-powered vehicles

These vehicles use animals. Animals pull the vehicles to make them move. Look at the dogs that pull this **sleigh**!

Machine-powered vehicles

These vehicles have a **motor**. The motor makes them move. Look at this airplane. It can take us to faraway places!

2 **Listen and read. Which vehicle is machine-powered?**

Did You Know?
People first used boats around 8,000 years ago!

Read and Learn

1 Look and label.

airplane sleigh canoe bike

1 ....

2 ....

3 ....

4 ....

2 Read and circle.

1 A **sleigh** / **bike** is a human-powered vehicle.

2 An **airplane** / **canoe** is a machine-powered vehicle.

3 A **car** / **sleigh** is an animal-powered vehicle.

3 Ask and answer with a friend. Use words from the box.

school the mall the movie theater the park

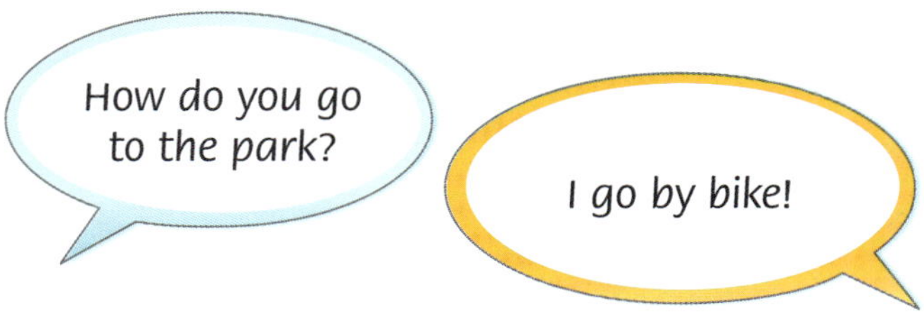

Time to Think

1 Look and complete.

1 ___Frank___ is using an animal-powered vehicle.

2 ______________ is not using a vehicle.

3 ______________ is using a vehicle with a motor.

4 ______________ and ______________ are using human-powered vehicles.

2 Read and match.

1 Bikes

2 Sleighs

3 Buses

a can travel on snow.

b can help us do exercise.

c can carry lots of people at the same time.

3 Read and complete.

park bike human-powered exercise

This is my 1 ______________! It's a 2 ______________ vehicle. I use it to go to the 3 ______________. It helps me do some 4 ______________!

Project

Prepare and Create

1 Work together and follow the instructions.

1 Invent a new vehicle. It can be human-powered, animal-powered, or machine-powered.

2 Make a poster of your new vehicle.

Showcase

2 Share your vehicle with the class.

It's Our World

Do you like to walk? Where do you walk?

Chapter 6 Adopt a Pet!

Social Sciences

1 Look at the pictures. What do you think the text is about?

Friends Forever!

Do you want to **adopt** a pet? Visit an animal shelter!

Animal shelters have different types of pets. They have big pets and small pets, including cats, dogs, turtles, birds, and many others!

The pets are all waiting for a family to love them and take care of them!

How do you take care of a pet?

Feed it and give it water!

Brush its hair!

Walk it every day!

Clean its **litter box**!

Clean its **cage**!

Take it to the **vet**!

2 Listen and read. What pet needs to go out for a walk?

Read and Learn

1 Look and circle.

1 play / brush **2** walk / vet **3** feed / clean **4** cage / litter box

2 Read and write Yes or No.

1 Do you brush a turtle and play with it? ....

2 Do you feed a cat and clean his litter box? ....

3 Do you clean a bird's cage and take him to the vet? ....

4 Do you walk a hamster? ....

3 Ask and answer with a friend.

Do you have a dog?

Yes, I do.

Did You Know?

People in ancient Egypt had many pets, including cats, dogs, monkeys, and crocodiles.

Time to Think

1 Read and answer.

	Monday	Tuesday	Wednesday	Thursday	Friday
Feed Pepe	John	Anna	Anna	Mom	John
Brush Pepe	Anna	Mom	John	John	Dad
Walk Pepe	Dad	John	Dad	John	Anna

1 Who feeds Pepe every Tuesday and Wednesday? ______

2 Who doesn't walk Pepe? ______

3 Who brushes Pepe and walks Pepe on the same day? ______

2 Look at Activity 1. Then read and complete.

I help take care of Pepe every week!
I **1** ___feed___ him on Tuesday and Wednesday. On Monday I **2** ______ his hair, and on Friday I **3** ______ him in the park. And I play with him every day!

Anna and Pepe

Project

Prepare and Create

1 Work together and follow the instructions.

1 Think of a pet you want to adopt.

2 Make a poster showing how you take care of your new pet.

Showcase

2 Share your poster with the class.

It's Our World

Is it okay to have any animal as a pet?

Chapter 7

The Night Sky

Science

1 **Look at the title. What do you think the text is about?**

Pictures in the Sky

Look at the **stars** in the **sky**. Some of them make pictures.

When a group of stars makes a picture, it is called a **constellation**. There are 88 constellations. Some look like people, some look like animals, and some look like things.

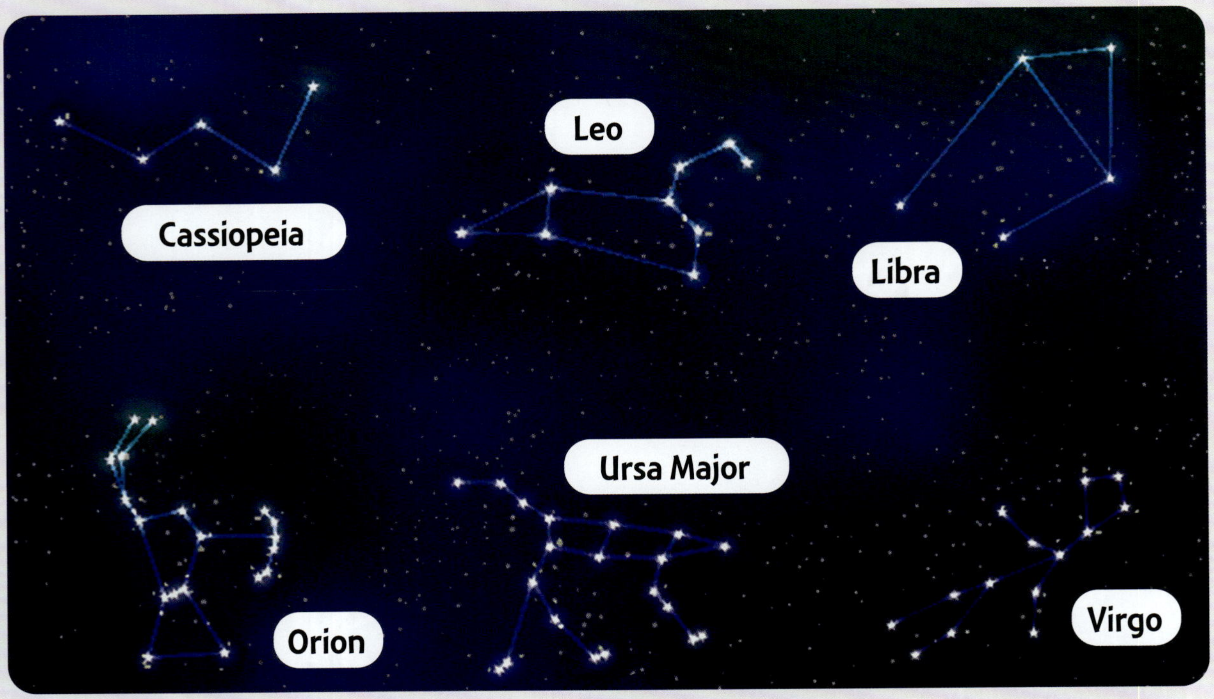

Orion **looks like** a hunter. What do you think he is hunting?

Ursa Major looks like a bear. Can you see the head, the body, and the legs?

Cassiopeia is a small constellation. It looks like the letter W.

2 **Listen and read. Which constellation looks like a letter of the alphabet?**

Did You Know?
The Sun is also a star.

Read and Learn

1 Complete and draw.

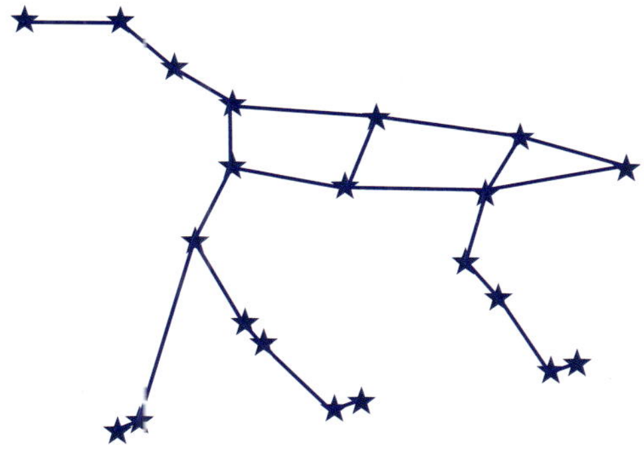

Orion looks like a hunter.   Ursa Major looks like a ....

2 Read and match.

1 What are constellations?

2 How many constellations are there?

3 What do constellations look like?

a There are 88.

b They are groups of stars that make pictures in the sky.

c They look like animals, people, or things.

3 Ask and answer with a friend.

Do you think Leo looks like a lion?

Yes, I think Leo looks like a lion.

No, I don't think Leo looks like a lion.

Time to Think

1 Read and complete.

animal   constellation   person   Virgo

Mia: Look! Which **1** .... is that?

Jack: Does it look like an **2** .... ?

Sam: No, it doesn't! It looks like a **3** .... !

Jack: It's **4** .... !

2 Look and draw and match.

What constellations can Mia, Jack, and Charlie see?

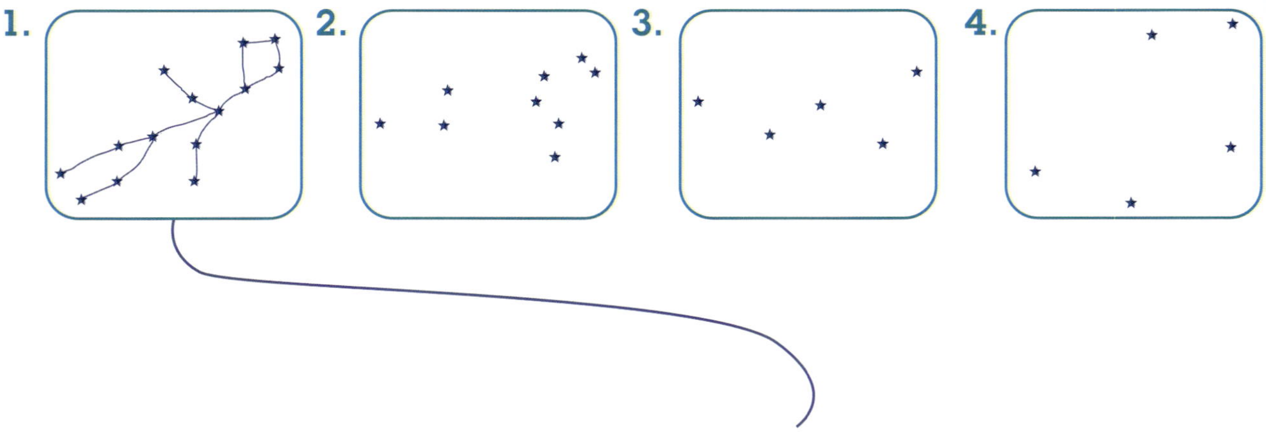

Libra   Cassiopeia   Virgo   Leo

Project

Prepare and Create

1 Work together and follow the instructions.

1 Choose two constellations from page 25 and two new constellations from the box.

2 Find out about the new constellations. Do they look like people, animals, or things?

3 Make a **Constellation Book** with pictures of the constellations you chose.

Cygnus
Hercules
Hydra
Pegasus
Perseus

Showcase

2 Share your Constellation Book with the class.

It's Our World
What animals do you see in the stars?

Chapter 8

From Farm to Plate

Home Economics

1 Look at the title and the pictures. What do you think the text is about?

Where does our food come from?

We buy our food in a **supermarket**, but where does it come from? Most food comes from a **farm** or a **factory**.

Food that comes directly from a farm is called **natural food**. Broccoli and chicken are natural foods.

Food that comes from a factory is called **processed food**. Pizza and ice-cream are processed foods.

Farmers produce **ingredients** like meat and vegetables. Then a factory uses the ingredients to make processed food.

2 Listen and read. What kind of food comes from a factory?

1 Unscramble and label.

mfra stingedrein ~~tekrsamruep~~ yaroftc

1 supermarket 2 ________ 3 ________ 4 ________

2 Read and write T (True) or F (False).

1 Farmers produce pizza. ____

2 People can buy natural and processed foods from a supermarket. ____

3 Trucks take ingredients from a farm to a factory. ____

4 Farmers use ingredients from a factory to make food. ____

3 Ask and answer with a friend.

What natural foods do you eat?

I eat chicken.

Did You Know?
Pasta is a processed food. It can last for up to 30 years!

Time to Think

1 Write the foods in the correct categories.

cake ~~fish~~ fries milk pasta peas

Natural Foods	Processed Foods
fish	

2 Read and complete.

farm fish natural salad

Hi! My name's Ben. I like to eat **1** ______ and **2** ______ . They come directly from the **3** ______ . They are **4** ______ and they are healthy. What foods do you like to eat?

3 What foods do you like to eat? Answer.

1 What processed foods do you like to eat?

____

2 What natural foods do you like to eat?

____

Project

Prepare and Create

1 Work together and follow the instructions.

1 Look for pictures of food that comes from a farm or a factory.

2 Make a poster that shows the differences.

Showcase

2 Share your poster with the class.

It's Our World

Do you eat food from different countries?

Chapter 9

Let's Get Active!

Social Sciences

1 Look at the pictures. Do you know any of the activities?

Exercise to the Rhythm of Music!

Music helps athletes concentrate, move to the rhythm, and have fun! Here are some sports that combine music and movement.

Capoeira is a combination of martial arts and dance. Capoeira athletes **flip over** and spin.

Artistic swimming is a combination of swimming and dance. Artistic swimmers swim and **spin** in the water.

Figure skating is a combination of skating and dance. Figure skaters skate, **jump**, and spin on the ice!

jump

flip over

spin

2 Listen and read. What do artistic swimmers do?

Read and Learn

1 Look and write.

dance flip over ~~jump~~ spin

1

jump

2

....

3

....

4

....

2 Read and complete.

artistic swimming capoeira figure skating

1 In .... you jump and spin, but you don't flip over.

2 In .... you flip over and spin, but you don't jump.

3 In .... you swim and spin, but you don't jump or skate.

3 Ask and answer with a friend.

What sport do you like?

I like capoeira.

Did You Know?
Before 1948, art and music competitions were included in the Olympic Games.

Time to Think

1 Look and write.

capoeira ~~figure skating~~ playing guitar
playing piano playing soccer

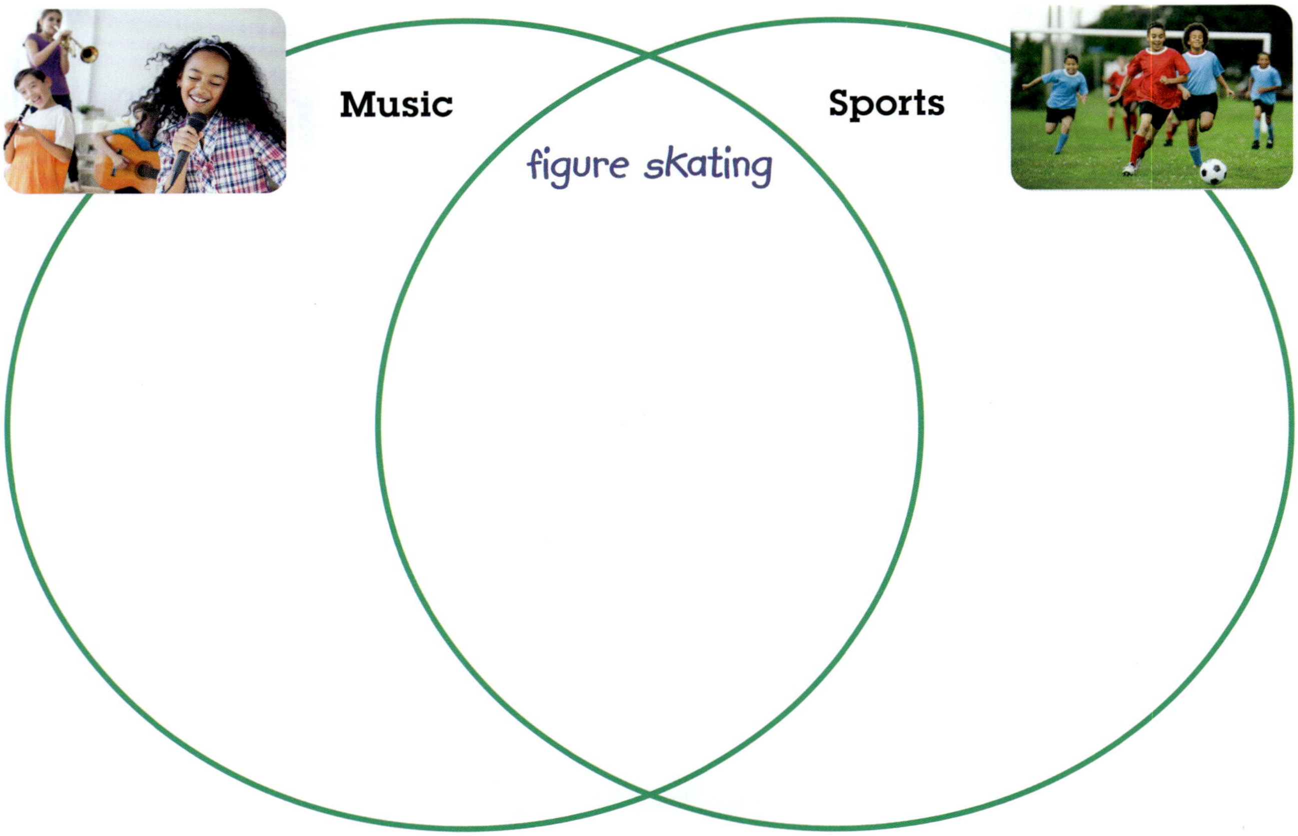

2 Work with a friend. Add three more activities to the chart in Activity 1.

3 Read and complete.

Two activities I like to do are ______________ and ______________.

One activity I would like to try is ______________.

Prepare and Create

1 Work together and follow the instructions.

1 Invent a new activity that combines music and sports.

2 Make a poster about your activity.

Showcase

2 Share your poster with the class.

It's Our World

What sports are popular in your country?

Macmillan Education Limited
4 Crinan Street
London N1 9XW

Companies and representatives throughout the world

Story Central Plus Level 1 CLIL Book ISBN 978-1-380-06085-3
Story Central Plus Level 1 Student Book with Reader, CLIL Book, Student eBook, Reader eBook, and CLIL eBook
ISBN 978-1-380-06082-2

Written by L. Peimbert.

This edition published 2021
First edition entitled "Story Central" published 2015 by Macmillan Education Limited

Designed by Composure based on an original design by Liz Adock.
Page make-up by Composure.
Illustrated by Beth Hughes (The Bright Agency) pp 6(b), 7, 8(bl, br), 9(b1), 10, 11, 15, 19, 22, 23, 27, 29, 31, 32(bc), 33(2), 35, 39.
Cover design by Wild Apple Design Ltd. and Roberto Martinez
Cover illustration Steven Wood (Advocate Art)
Cover photographs by **Getty Images**/jhorrocksv, **Macmillan Education Limited**/Getty Images/BJI/Blue Jean Images
Picture research by Luz Cordero

The authors and publishers would like to thank the following for permission to reproduce their photographs:
Alamy Stock Photo/Jonathan Ball p. 18(snow chair), Alamy Stock Photo/Jon G. Fuller, Jr. p. 18(stone bed);
Getty Images/borchee pp. 4(tl), 5(l), Getty Images/bortonia pp. 28(c), 29, 30, Getty Images/fotogaby pp. 20(sleigh), 21(1), Getty Images/Kilito Chan p. 8(background), Getty Images/jhorrocksv p. 16(brick house), Getty Images/LOVE_LIFE pp. 4(tr), 5(cr), Getty Images/MirageC p. 36(background), Getty Images/Thomas Winz p. 20(background), Getty Images/SeventyFour p. 36(cl), Getty Images/Xinzheng p.18(brick floor); **Macmillan Education Limited**/Alamy Images Stock Photo/imageBROKER p. 13(monkey), Macmillan Education Limited/Alamy Stock Photo/Radius Images pp. 16(wood), 17(r), Macmillan Education Limited/Alamy Stock Photo/M. Timothy O'Keefe p. 13(parrot), Macmillan Education Limited/Getty Images/4kodiak p. 28(background), Macmillan Education Limited/Getty Images/500px Prime/Aivaras Grauzinis p. 13(crocodile), Macmillan Education Limited/Getty Images/anankkml p. 14(leopard), Macmillan Education Limited/Getty Images/Tony Anderson p. 16(cabin), Macmillan Education Limited/Getty Images/BJI/Blue Jean Images pp. 24(tr), 25(2), Macmillan Education Limited/Getty Images/blackred p. 14(apple), Macmillan Education Limited/Getty Images/Aaron Foster pp. 20(plane), 21(3), Macmillan Education Limited/Getty Images/Fuse p. 24(br), Macmillan Education Limited/Getty Images/fStop/Liesel Bockl pp. 4(bl), 5(r), Macmillan Education Limited/Getty Images/gbh007 p. 22, Macmillan Education Limited/Getty Images/Chris Hepburn pp. 16(stone), 17(cr), Macmillan Education Limited/Getty Images/Blend Images/JGI/Jamie Grill,JGI/Jamie Grill/Blend Images p. 38(cr), Macmillan Education Limited/Getty Images/kajakiki pp. 32(background), Macmillan Education Limited/Getty Images/Kwanchai Lerttanapunyaporn/EyeEm p. 14(butterfly), Macmillan Education Limited/Getty Images/mbbirdy pp. 16(snow), 17(l), Macmillan Education Limited/Getty Images/Maciej Nicgorski/EyeEm pp. 32(bl), 33(cr), Macmillan Education Limited/Getty Images/ozgurdonmaz p. 34(cl), Macmillan Education Limited/Getty Images/RooM RF/meaghanbrowning p. 24(background), Macmillan Education Limited/Getty Images/Pakin Songmor p. 14(tree), Macmillan Education Limited/Getty Images/ssucsy pp. 16(brick wall), 17(cl), Macmillan Education Limited/Getty Images/Valeriy_G p. 26, Macmillan Education Limited/Getty Images/Westend61/Fotofeeling p. 13(elephant), Macmillan Education Limited/Getty Images/Westend61/Jan Börner pp. 20(canoe), 21(2), Macmillan Education Limited/Getty Images/xxmmxx pp. 4(br), 5(cl), Macmillan Education Limited/Getty Images/iStockphoto/1001slide p. 12(background), Macmillan Education Limited/Getty Images/iStockphoto/FatCamera p. 38(cl), Macmillan Education Limited/iStockphoto/jamesdvdsn p. 14(spider), Macmillan Education Limited/Getty Images/iStockphoto/jaochainoi p. 4(background), Macmillan Education Limited/Getty Images/iStockphoto/mddphoto p. 14(giraffe), Macmillan Education Limited/iStockphoto/Smitt p. 16(igloo); **Shutterstock**/New Africa pp. 24(bl), 25(4) Shutterstock/A. PAES p. 36(tl), Shutterstock/EniSine p. 24(bc), Shutterstock/Koltsov pp. 24(tc), 25(1), Shutterstock/Microgen p. 36(cr), Shutterstock/Christian Mueller p. 24(tl), 25(3), Shutterstock/nuttakit p. 18(wooden desk), Shutterstock/Smit p. 16(background).

Printed and bound in Brazil.
2025
10

Story Central Plus

Student Book 1 with eBook

Viv Lambert
Mo Choy

macmillan education

Contents

Competencies

me	act	think	learn	communicate
Activities that encourage children to accept responsibility and reflect on the consequences of lifestyle choices.	Activities that develop societal understanding and identification of children's own circumstances in a wider context.	Activities that develop critical thinking skills to reflect upon, manipulate, process, and interpret information.	Activities that foster learner autonomy, and allow children to demonstrate and put into practice learning strategies.	Activities that promote interpersonal and collaborative skills, develop teamwork, and allow children to express opinions and ideas.

Story Central

1 Listen and sing.

Welcome, Welcome

Welcome, welcome, everyone!
Story Central is a lot of fun.

Please come in and close the door.
Sit on a chair, sit on the floor.

Welcome, welcome, everyone!
Story Central is a lot of fun.

Walk around and take a look.
Watch a show, choose a book.

Welcome, welcome, everyone!
Story Central is a lot of fun.

Read a poem, play a game.
Listen to a story, come again!

Welcome to Story Central

1 Listen and read. Then act out.

2 Listen and point. Then complete the blanks.

1 one
2 two
3 ....
4 four
5 five
6 six
7 ....
8 eight
9 nine
10 ....

....
yellow
....
green
pink
purple
....
black
....
white
gray

abc ....
efghij ....
lmno ....
qrst ....
vwxyz

3 Write about you.

Name: ....

Age: ....
Favorite color: ....

Grade: ....
Favorite number: ....

Teacher: ....
Favorite story: ....

Chapter 1

My School

Lesson 1

1 Listen and number. Then say.

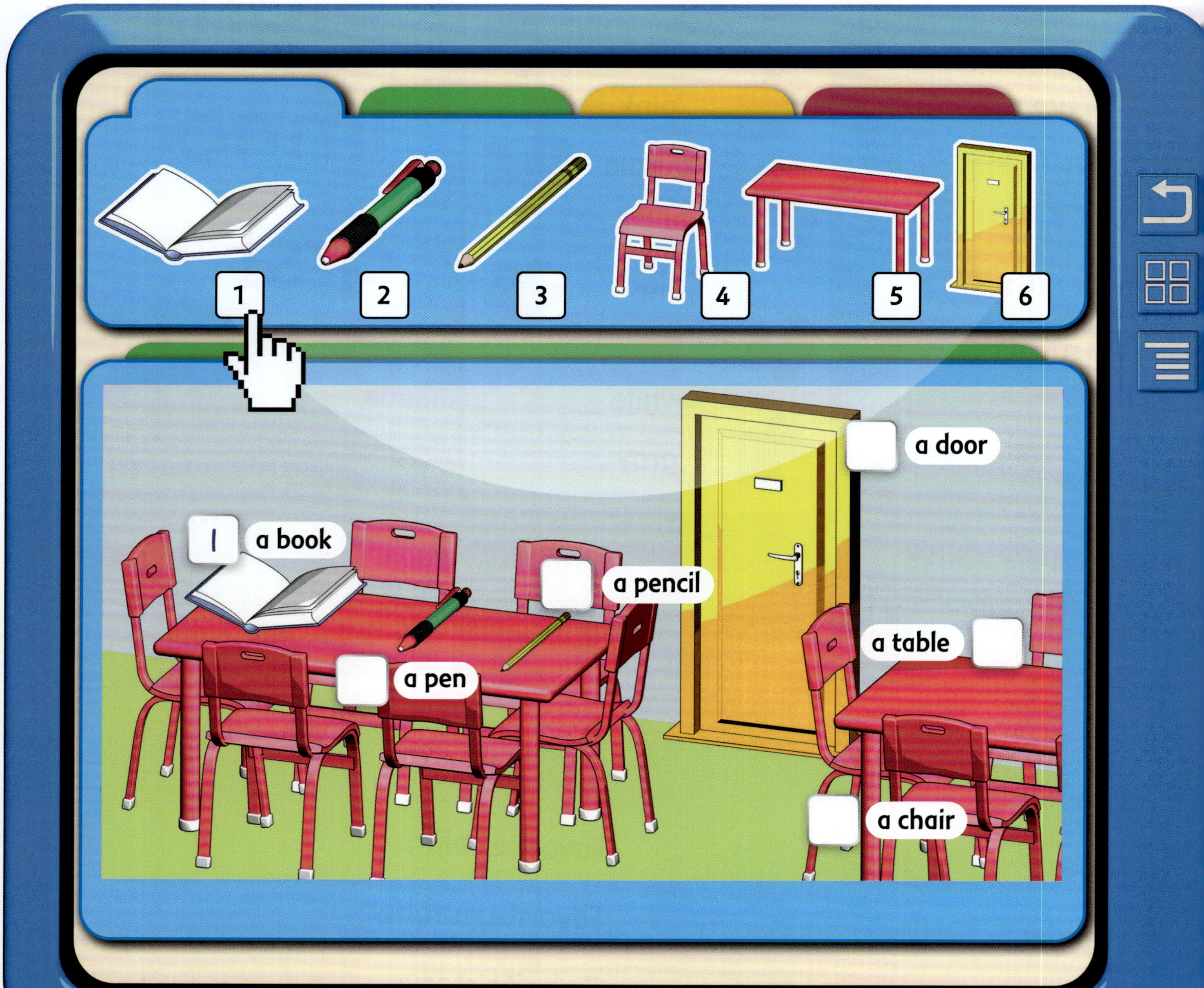

1 Complete the pictures. Then listen and number.

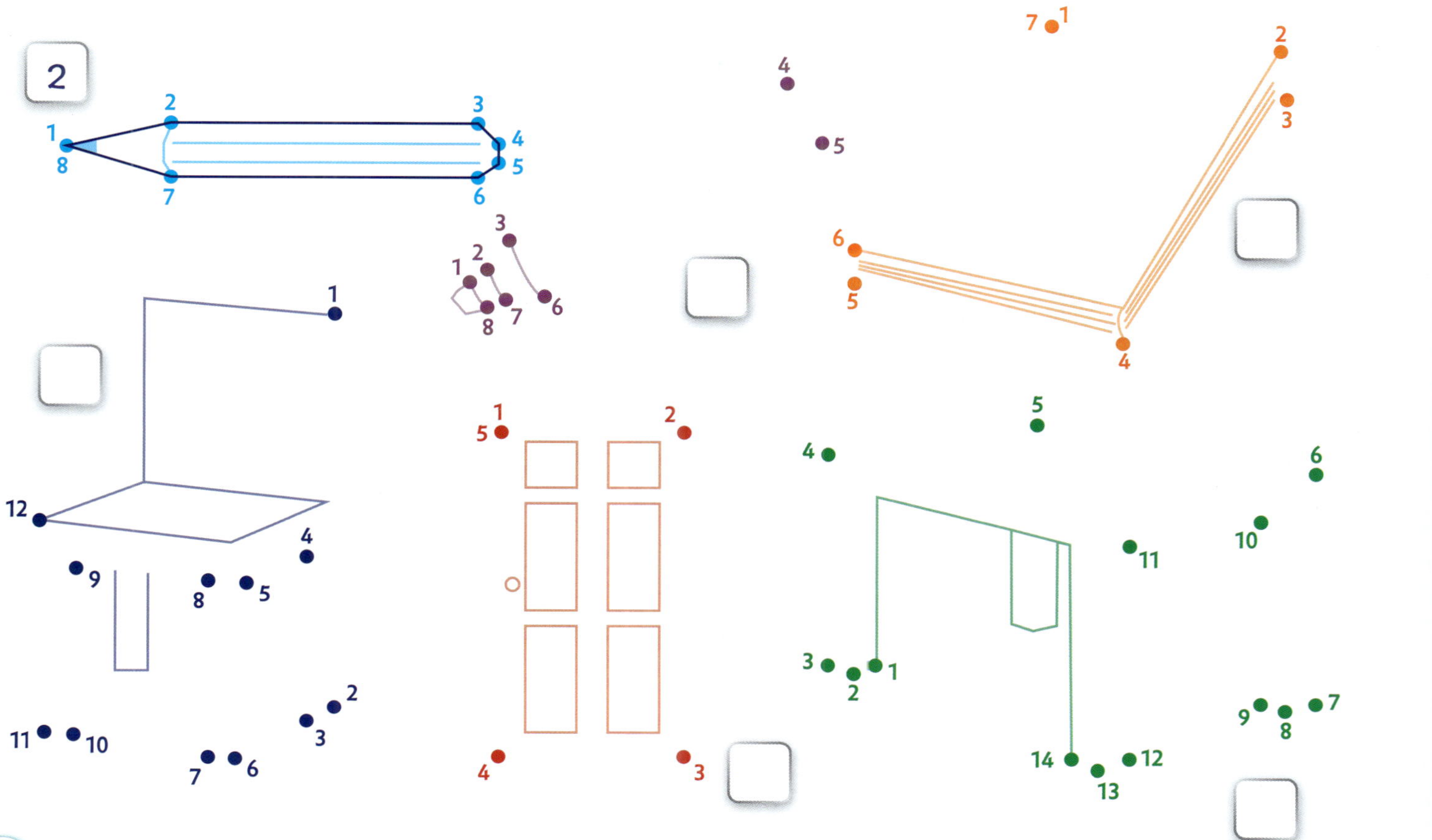

2 Point to the pictures. Ask and answer.

What is it?

It's a pencil.

3 Listen. Then play a guessing game.

Grammar Central

What is it? It's a pen.
Is it a pencil?
Yes, **it is**. / No, **it isn't**.

Grammar Booster on page 18

Lesson 3

1 Listen and read. Then act out.

2 Look at the story and think. What's it about?

3 Listen and read. What items are in the story?

a pen ☐ a chair ☐ a pencil ☐

a table ☐ a book ☐

Chen's Magic Pen

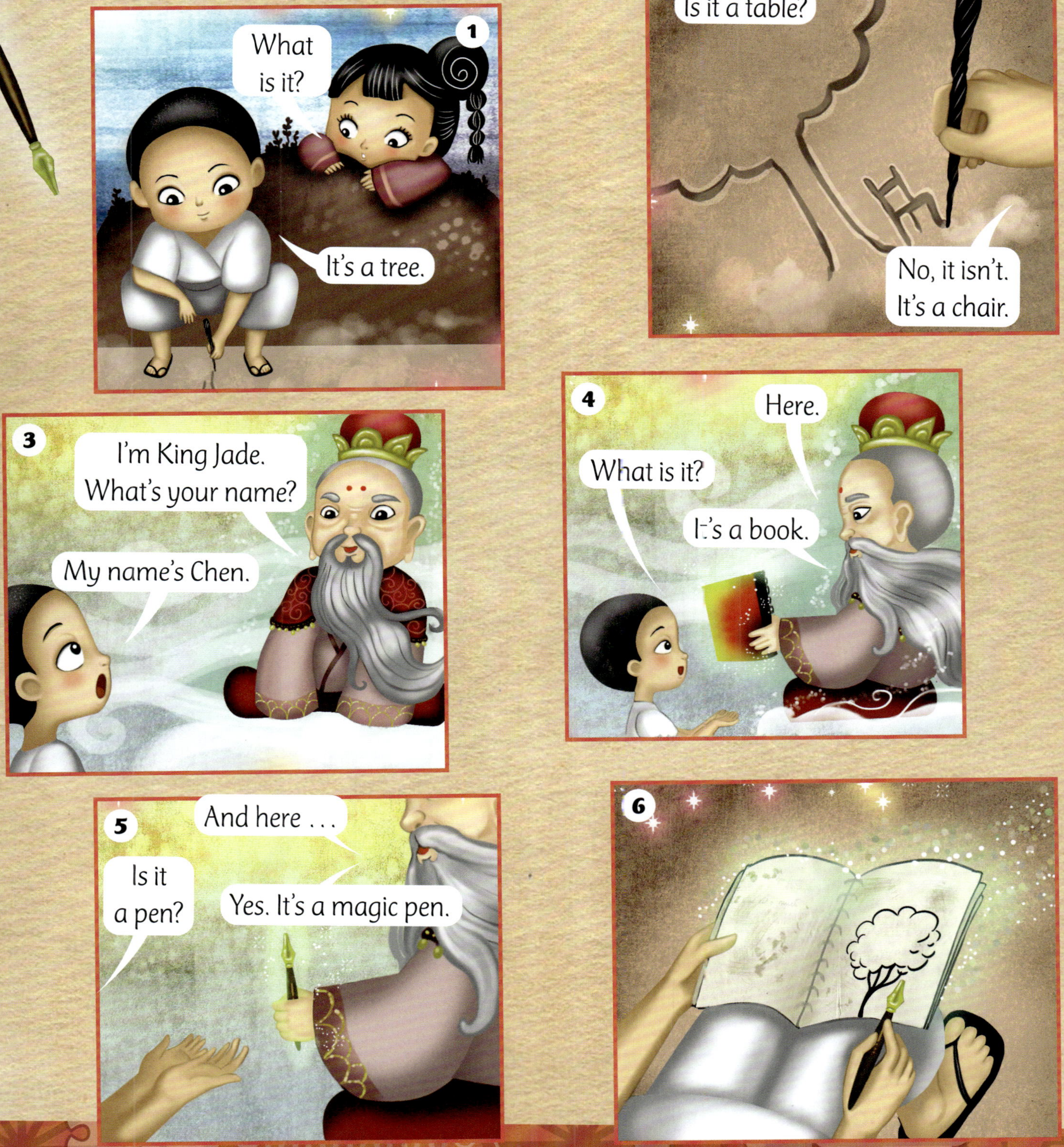

Reader Read the story in your Reader on pages 2–4.

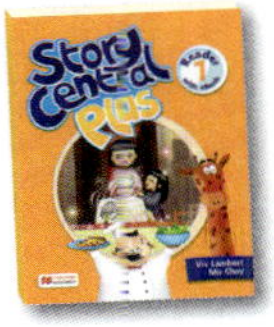

Lesson 4 Time to Think

1 Read the story in your Reader on pages 2–4 again.

I Can Read!

What's on the cover?

2 Check (✔) the items that Chen draws.

3 What would you ask Chen to draw?

4 Talk about the story.

Lesson 5

Song

1 Listen and match. Then sing.

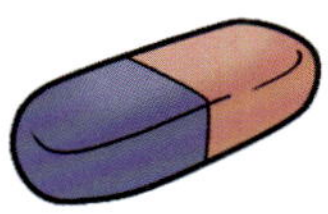

Thank You, Chen

Draw a bag, please,
With your magic pen.
Draw a crayon, please.
Thank you, Chen!

Draw a ruler, please,
With your magic pen.
Draw a pencil case, please.
Thank you, Chen!

Draw a notebook, please,
With your magic pen.
Draw an eraser, please.
Thank you, Chen!

2 Play a guessing game.

Is it an eraser?

Yes, it is.

3 Listen and say the chant.

Pen and pencil, pencil and pen.
Pink pencil, purple pen.

Lesson 6

1 Listen and read.

2 Answer the questions.

1 What color is the pen? It's blue.

2 What color is the notebook? ....

3 What's this? 

.... an eraser.

.... a pencil.

Grammar Central

What color is it?
It's green.
A blue pen. / **An orange** notebook.
It isn't a ruler.

Grammar Booster on page 19

1 Listen and read. Write the missing words.

2 Draw one more item on the tree.

3 Look at the tree. Ask and answer.

4 Class Vote!

Grow more trees. Yes or no?

Find Out More!

Why are trees important? Search the Internet or ask your teacher.

Project

Lesson 8

Prepare

1 Make a magic picture.

Showcase

2 Tell the story. Use your magic pictures.

1 Match the questions and answers.

1	What is it?	a	It's red.
2	Is it a bag?	b	I'm fine, thanks.
3	What color is it?	c	No, it isn't.
4	How are you?	d	It's an eraser.

2 Listen and circle. Then write.

1 a red ruler
2
3
4
5
6

3 Think about Chapter 1. Color the books.

Treasure Hunt!

Look back at pages 4 and 5. Find:

a purple notebook

Grammar Booster

What is it?

1 Read and complete.

Use ***What is it?*** or ***Is it a …?*** to ask what an object is.

Question	Answer
What 1 is it ?	2 ________ a pen.
3 ________ is it?	It's a crayon.

Question	Answer
4 ________ a chair?	Yes, it is.
Is it a ruler?	No, it 5 ________.

it's = it is
it isn't = it is not

2 Look and write.

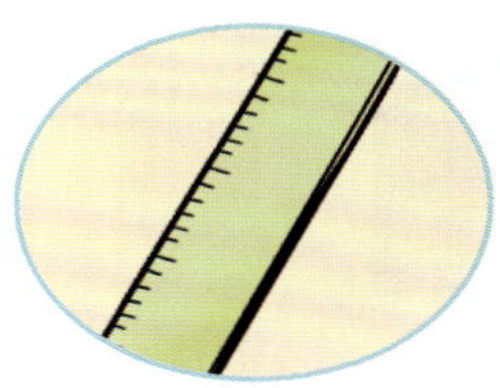

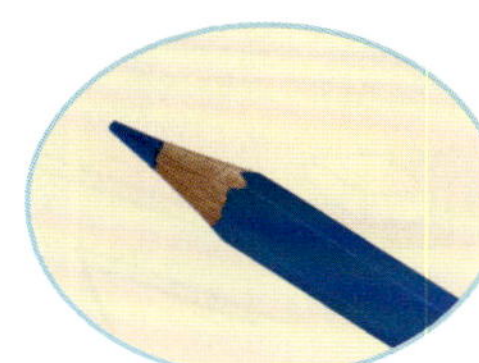

1 What is it?

It's a table.

2 What is it?

____

3 Is it a pencil?

____

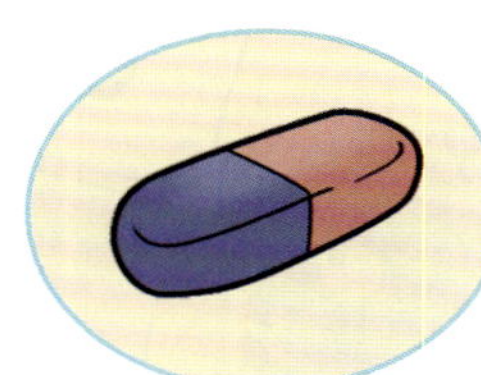

4 Is it an eraser?

____

5 ________

It's a notebook.

6 ________

No, it isn't.

What color is it?

1 Read and complete.

Use ***What color is it?*** to ask what color an object is.

Question	Answer	
What color 1 ___is it___?	It's green.	It's a green notebook.
2 ________ color is it?	It's orange.	3 ________ an orange ruler.

Use ***It's a/an*** … or ***It isn't a/an*** … to describe an object.

Positive ✔	Negative ✘
It's a book.	It 4 ________ a pencil.
It's 5 ________ apple.	It isn't a banana.

a banana / **an** apple

2 Look and color. Then complete.

1 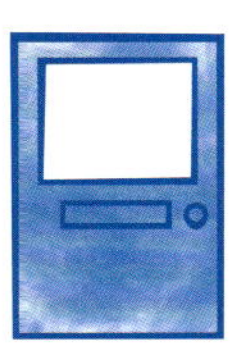

2 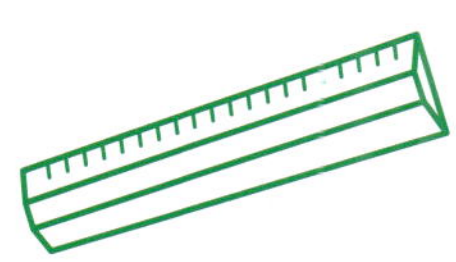

3 

1 What ___color___ is it?

It's blue. ________ a blue door. It ________ a red door.

2 ________ color is it?

________ green. ________ a green ruler. ________ a green pencil.

3 ________________ is it?

________ orange. ________ orange pencil case. ________ a blue eraser.

Grammar Review

1 Read and complete.

2 Look and answer.

1 Is it a bag? No, it isn't.

2 What is it? ________

3 What color is it? ________

4 Is it a door? ________

5 Is it a table? ________

Grammar Challenge

1 Find and circle. Then write.

1 What is it? — It's an apple.

2 What is it? — ________ a ruler.

3 ________ is it? — It's brown.

4 ________ an eraser? — No, ________.

5 What's his ________? — His ________ David.

6 ________ is she? — She's ________.

1

2

3

4

5

6

2 Find one more object in the picture. Write two questions. Now ask a friend.

1 ________________ ________________

2 ________________ ________________

It's My World!

What's in your school bag? What's your favorite color? Ask a friend.

Chapter 2 My Toys

Lesson 1

1 Listen and write the letter. Then say.

TOYS

a

b

c
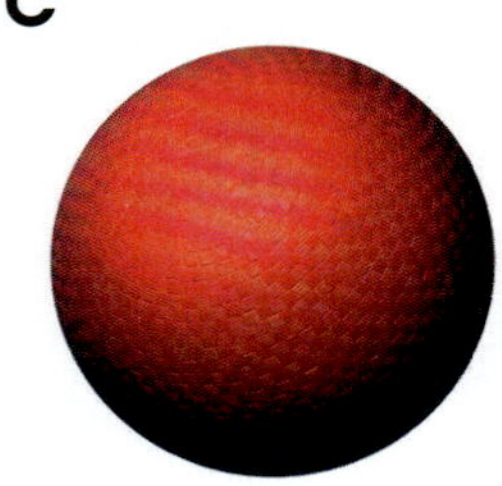

f

d

e

a a car	**b** a robot	**c** a ball
d a doll	**e** a bike	**f** a teddy bear

My Birthday List

a robot	b
a doll	
a teddy bear	
a car	
a bike	
a ball	

1 Listen and point.

2 Listen again and circle. Then check with a friend.

1 This is / That's my ball.

2 This is / That's my car.

3 This is / That's my robot.

4 This is / That's my teddy bear.

3 Listen. Then ask and answer.

Grammar Central

This is **my** doll.
That's **my** bike.
Is **this your** bike?
Is **that your** doll?

Grammar Booster on page 32

Lesson 3

1 Listen and read. Then act out.

2 Look at the story and think. What's it about?

3 Listen and read. What items are in the story?

a teddy bear ☐ a bike ☐ a car ☐

The Princess and the Teddy Bear

Reader Read the story in your Reader on pages 5–7.

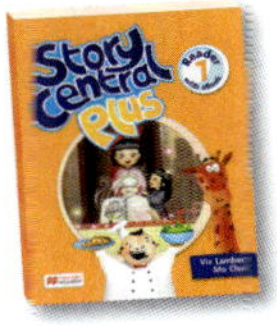

Lesson 4 Time to Think

1 Read the story in your Reader on pages 5–7 again.

I Can Read!

What's on the cover?

2 Check (✓) Princess Polly's teddy bear.

3 Draw something to give to Daisy.

4 Talk about the story.

Lesson 5

Song

1 Listen and point. Then sing and shout your name.

December January November February October March September April August May July June

When's Your Birthday?

January, February,
March, April, May.
June, July, August.
When's your birthday?

September, October,
Let's play a game.
November, December,
Shout out your name!

2 Class survey. Ask and answer.

When's your birthday?

It's in December.

3 Listen and say the chant.

June, July, or January?
January, July, or June?
When's your birthday?
Is it soon?

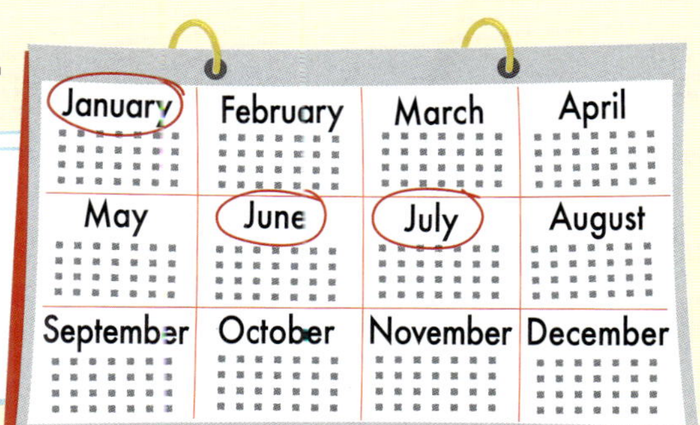

Lesson 6

1 Listen and read.

Happy Birthday, Tom!

2 Complete the blanks for Tom.

1 When's ___his___ birthday?
It's in ________.

2 How old is ________?
He's ________.

Grammar Centre

When's his birthday?
It's in April.
How old is he?
He's seven.

Grammar Booster on page 33

CLIL Math Lesson 7

1 Look and find shapes around you.

Shapes and Numbers

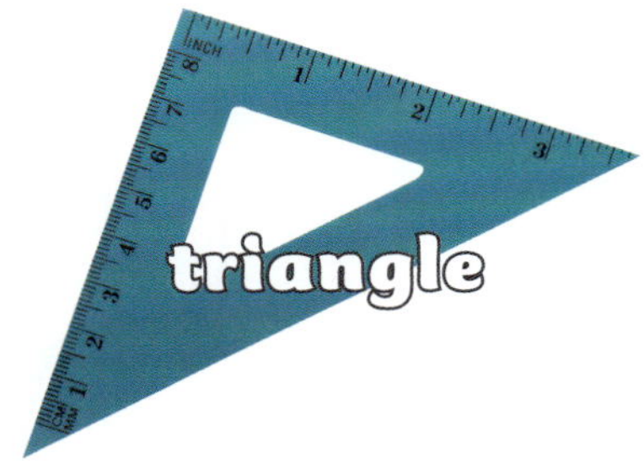

2 Listen and match. Then say.

thirteen eleven fifteen eighteen seventeen

fourteen twelve twenty sixteen nineteen

3 Look at the doll. Count and write.

4 Class Vote!

Math is fun! Yes or no?

Find Out More!
What other shapes are there? Search the Internet or ask your teacher.

Project

Lesson 8

Prepare

1 Make a toy poster.

Showcase

2 Tell the story. Use your posters.

1 Listen and check (✔) (Yes, it is.) or cross (✘) (No, it isn't.).

2 Look at the pictures. Complete the sentences.

1 She's 7. Her favorite toy is a teddy bear. Her name is ________________.

2 ________________ 17. ________________ birthday is in March. Her favorite toy is a robot. ________________ name is Libby.

3 Think about Chapter 2. Color the books.

Treasure Hunt!

Look back at pages 4 and 5. Find:

a ball

Grammar Booster

This and that

1 Read and complete.

Use ***this*** to talk about something that is near us and ***that*** to talk about something that is far away.

Near 	**Far** 
1 This is my robot.	2 ______ my teddy bear.
Is 3 ______ your robot?	Is 4 ______ your teddy bear?

that's = that is

2 Look and write.

How old are you?

1 Read and complete.

Use ***It's in*** + *month* to say when somebody's birthday is. Use ***How old are you?*** or ***How old is he/she?*** to ask somebody's age.

Question	Answer
When's your 1 birthday ?	It's 2 ______ September.
How old are 3 ______?	I'm seven.
4 ______ is she?	5 ______ ten.

2 Read and match. Then complete.

1 When's his birthday?

It's in July.

How old is he?

______

2 When's her birthday?

______

How old is she?

______

3 ______

It's in January.

______

He's nine.

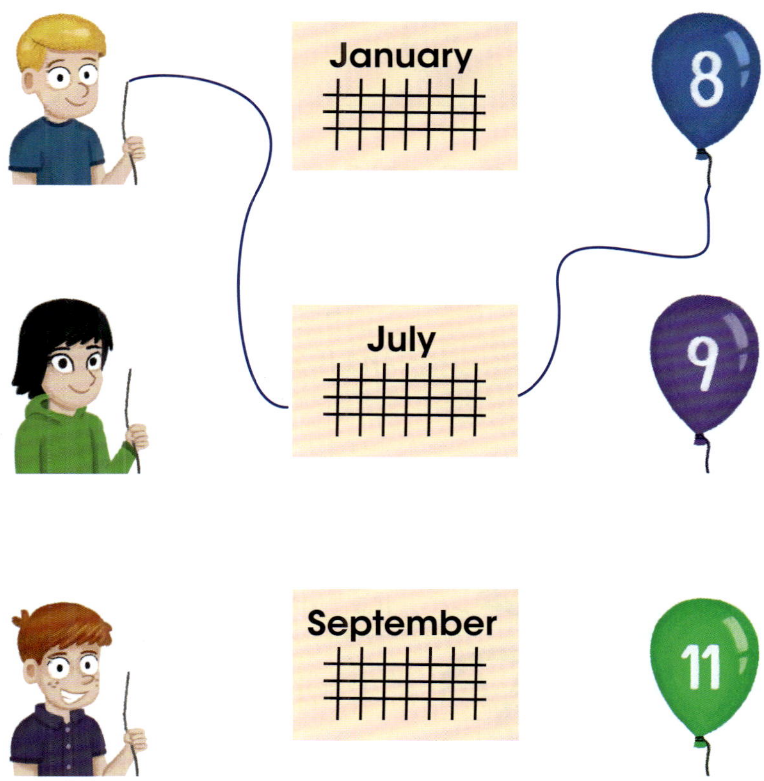

Grammar Review

1 Read, choose, and complete.

in   is   ~~that~~   This   When's

2 Read and circle.

1 **Write the missing words. Match and color.**

	Answer	Question
1	Yes, it is.	What is it?
2	It's green.	How ______ you?
3	It's ______ April.	How ______ is he?
4	I'm fine, thanks.	What's ______ favorite toy?
5	It's a robot.	What ______ is it?
6	It's a teddy bear.	When's his birthday?
7	No, it ______.	Is it a chair?
8	He's seven.	Is that your car?

2 **Write two more questions. Then ask a friend.**

1 ______________________________

2 ______________________________

It's My World!
When's your birthday? How old are you? Now ask a friend.

Chapter 3 Wild Animals

Lesson 1

1 Listen and number. Then say.

1 a giraffe
2 an elephant
3 a crocodile
4 a monkey
5 a lion
6 a tiger

1 Listen and point. Then say.

2 Listen and circle.

1 What are these?

They're tigers / monkeys.

2 What are those?

They're giraffes / elephants.

3 What are these?

They're monkeys / lions.

4 What are those?

They're crocodiles / elephants.

3 Now check with a friend.

What are these?

They're monkeys.

Grammar Central

What are these?
They're tigers.
What are those?
They're elephants.

Grammar Booster on page 46

Lesson 3

1 Listen and read. Then act out.

2 Look at the story and think. What's it about?

 ☐  ☐  ☐

3 Listen and read. What animals are in the story?

a giraffe ☐ an elephant ☐ a crocodile ☐

The Hungry Giraffe

Reader

Read the story in your Reader on pages 8–9.

Lesson 4 Time to Think

1 Read the story in your Reader on pages 8–9 again.

I Can Read!

Do you read from left to right ➡ or right to left ⬅ ?

2 Number the pictures in order.

3 Which friends do you share with?

I share with ....

4 Talk about the story.

Lesson 5

Song

1 Listen and point. Then sing.

Happy Giraffe

Look at those scary tigers!
They're orange, black, and white.
They're very scary tigers.
And they're hungry tonight.

Look at these snappy crocodiles!
They're long and they're green.
They're snappy, snappy crocodiles.
With big scary teeth!

I'm a happy giraffe.
I'm thin and I'm tall.
I love these green leaves.
I'm not hungry at all.

2 Play a guessing game.

tall long thin scary hungry

They're long and green.

They're crocodiles!

3 Listen and say the chant.

We're tall. We're thin. We're tall and thin. Two giraffes are tall and thin.

Lesson 6

1 Listen and read.

2 Write Tom's answers.

1 Is it a crocodile? No, it isn't.

2 Is it a spider? ____________.

3 Are monkeys scary? ____________.

4 Are spiders scary? ____________.

Grammar Centr

Spiders **aren't** scary.
Are monkeys scary?
Yes, **they are**. /
No, **they aren't**.

Grammar Booster on page 47

1 Listen and read.

Hungry Animals

Look at these **giraffes**. They're tall. They eat leaves from these tall trees.

These animals are **zebras**! They aren't tall. They eat grass. **Elephants** eat grass and leaves, too.

What's this? It's a **leopard**. Leopards eat meat. **Lions** eat meat, too. Watch out, zebras! Those lions are scary. They eat zebras and other animals.

Some animals eat meat and some animals eat grass, fruit, and leaves. **Monkeys** eat meat and fruit. What do you eat?

2 Write the animals in the correct places.

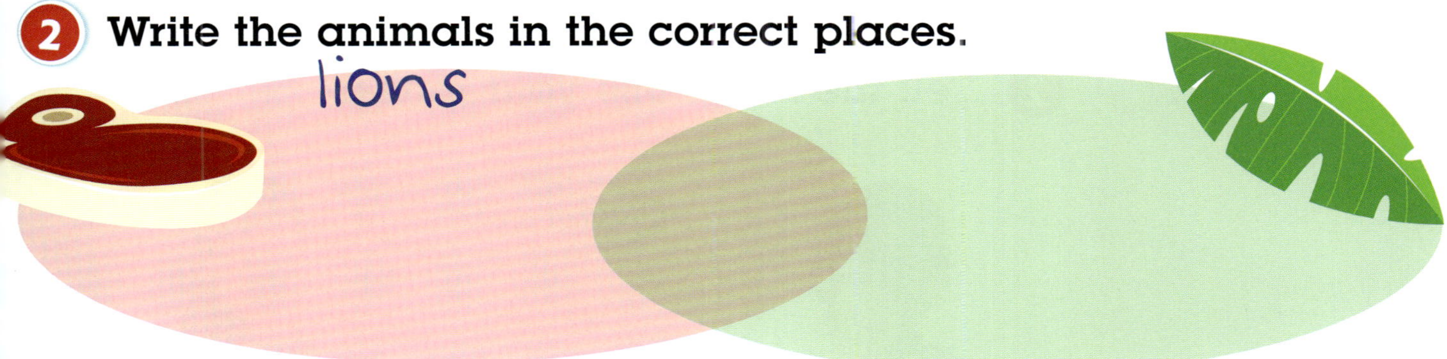

3 Class Vote!

Leopards are scary. Yes or no?

Find Out More!

Choose an animal. Find out what it eats. Search the Internet or ask your teacher.

Project

Lesson 8

Prepare

1 Choose a mask to make.

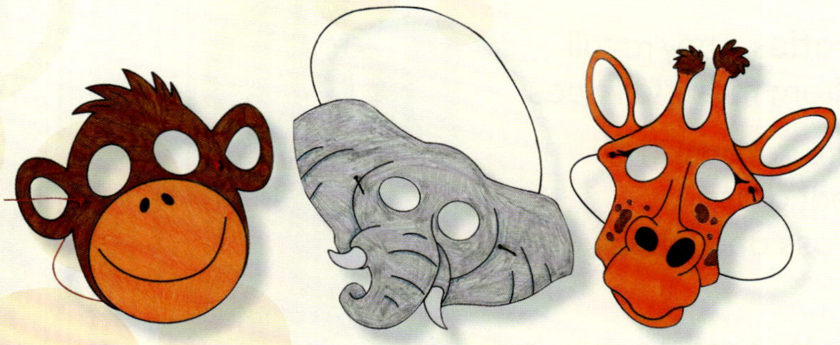

Showcase

2 Tell the story. Use your masks.

Review

1 Look and complete the blanks.

1 What are these? They're elephants.
2 What ______? ______ lions.
3 What are those? They're ______.
4 ______ are those? ______ tigers.

2 Circle the correct answer.

1 Are crocodiles long and green? Yes, they are. / No, they aren't.
2 Are lions scary? Yes, they are. / Yes, it is.
3 Are giraffes small? Yes, they are. / No, they aren't.
4 Are spiders tall? No, it isn't. / No, they aren't.

3 Think about Chapter 3. Color the books.

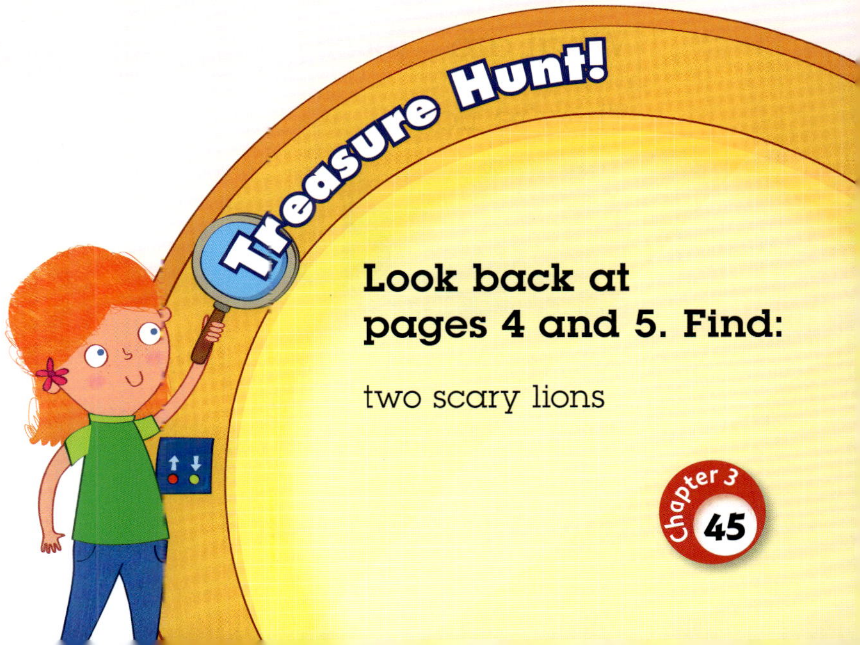

Look back at pages 4 and 5. Find:

two scary lions

Grammar Booster

These and those

1 Read and complete.

Use the plural (*noun* + ***s***) for more than one person or thing.

Singular (one)			Plural (more than one)		
1 book	friend	2 ______	books	3 ______	lions

Use ***these*** to talk about things that are near us and ***those*** to talk about things that are far away.

Near	Far

What are 4 ______?	What are 5 ______?
They're crocodiles.	They're tigers.

they**'re** = they are

2 Complete the sentences.

1 What are those?

They're lions.

2 What are these?

______ elephants.

3 What ______?

______ monkeys.

4 What ______?

______ crocodiles.

They are and they aren't

1 Read and complete.

Use ***They're*** + *adjective* or
They aren't + *adjective* to describe people or things.

Use ***Are they*** + *adjective*? to ask about people or things.

Positive ✔	Negative ✘
1 They're hungry.	2 They ______ scary.
Question	**Short answer ✔ ✘**
3 ______ green?	Yes, they 4 ______. No, they 5 ______.

they**'re** = they are
they **aren't** = they are not

2 Read and answer. What do you think?

1 Are elephants thin? No, they aren't.
2 Are monkeys cute? ______
3 Are teddy bears scary? ______
4 Are bananas long? ______
5 Are crocodiles green? ______
6 Are giraffes tall? ______

Grammar Review

1 Read and number the pictures in the correct order.

2 Read again then answer.

1 Are they happy?

---

2 What's this?

---

3 Are they hungry?

---

4 What are those?

---

5 Is she happy?

Grammar Challenge

1 Choose and write the missing words. Then answer.

scary   eat   They're   ~~Those~~   yellow   That

1 Those animals are leopards. 2 .... black and
3 .... They're big and 4 .... Look at their teeth!
5 .... animal is a zebra. Watch out, zebra! Leopards
6 .... zebras!

2 Now make sentences about Leo and Leila.

1 These leopards / big.
These leopards aren't big.

2 They / scary.
....

3 They / cute.
....

4 Their names / Leo and Leila.
....

5 They / my favorite toys.
....

It's My World!
What's your favorite animal?
Why? Now ask a friend.

Chapter 4 My House

Lesson 1

1 Listen and number. Then say.

1 Listen and number. Then say.

in the bag

under the table

behind the door

on the chair

2 Now look again. Where's the mouse? Listen and circle the correct answer.

1 It's behind / in the bag.

2 It's on / under the chair.

3 It's under / on the table.

4 It's on / behind the cat.

3 Ask and answer.

Grammar Central

Where's the cat?
It's **in** the living room.
It's **behind** the door.

Grammar Booster on page 60

Lesson 3

1 Listen and read. Then act out.

2 Look at the story and think. What's it about?

3 Listen and read. What rooms are in the story?

kitchen ☐ bathroom ☐ living room ☐

THE MYSTERY HOUSE

Reader

Read the story in your Reader on pages 10–13.

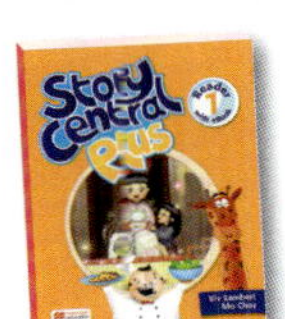

1 Read the story in your Reader on pages 10–13 again.

I Can Read!
When do we use these?

2 Number the rooms in order.

3 Draw something valuable.

4 Talk about the story.

Lesson 5

Song

1 Listen and find the shoe. Then sing.

One Shoe is Missing

One shoe is missing.
It's a mystery.
One shoe is missing.
Help me find it, please!

It isn't in the bedroom,
Under the bed.
It isn't in the closet,
Or under the desk.

It isn't in the kitchen.
It isn't on the floor.
It isn't in the garage,
On the shelf behind the door.

It isn't in the living room,
Behind the TV,
Or under the sofa.
Help me find it, please!

2 Ask and answer.

Where's the ball?

It's under the bed.

3 Listen and say the chant.

A ruler, a ruler. A long, red ruler.
A long, red ruler in the living room.

Lesson 6

1 Listen and read.

2 Look at the story. Circle the correct words.

1 Stand up / Don't stand up tall.
2 What can you see / say?
3 Sit down / Don't sit down on the sofa.
4 The prize begins with c / e / g.

Grammar Centre

Stand up.
Don't sit down.
Open the book.

Grammar Booster on page 61

1 Listen and read.

Different Homes

What is a home? Where you live is your home. Do you live in a house or an apartment? Look at this boat. It's a home, too. It's a houseboat!

Take a look. The kitchen is in the living room. The bedroom is in the living room, too. At night, the sofa is a bed. Where's the TV? It's on the shelf. Is that a closet? No, it's a bathroom.

2 Circle T (true) or F (false).

1 The bedroom is in the living room. T / F
2 The sofa is a bed. T / F
3 The TV is on the shelf. T / F
4 The TV is under the desk. T / F
5 The bathroom is in the kitchen. T / F
6 The kitchen is in the closet. T / F

3 Class Vote!

House or houseboat?

Find Out More!
Find more unusual houses. Search the Internet or ask your teacher.

Project

Lesson 8

Prepare

1 Make a mystery house.

Showcase

2 Tell the story. Use your mystery house.

1 Listen and draw lines. Then write.

1 The doll is on the bed.
2 The bag is ....
3 The cat is ....
4 The car is ....

2 Choose the correct instruction. Then write.

Come in. Don't sit down. Open the door.

....

3 Think about Chapter 4. Color the books.

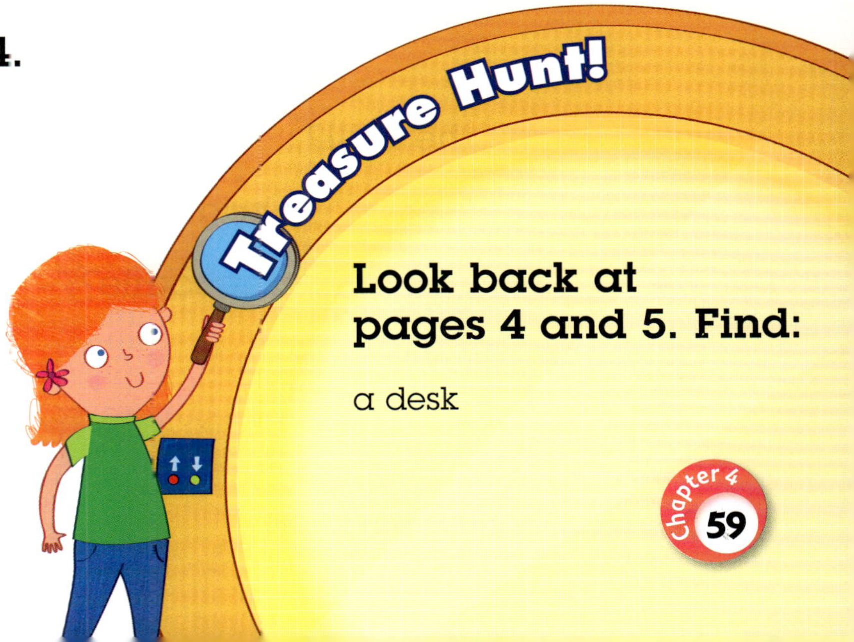

Look back at pages 4 and 5. Find:

a desk

Grammar Booster

Where is it?

1 Read and complete.

Use ***Where's the …?*** to ask where something is. To answer, use ***It's behind / in / on / under*** + *noun*.

1 __________ the ball?

It's **2** ___in___ the bag.

It's **3** __________ the table.

It's **4** __________ the table.

It's **5** __________ the bag.

Where'**s** = Where is

2 Look and write.

1 Where's the doll?

___It's under the___ chair.

2 Where's the robot?

__________ chair.

3 Where's the ball?

__________ bag.

4 __________ crocodile?

It's under the bed.

5 __________ bag?

It's on the bed.

6 __________ teddy bear?

It's behind the chair.

Instructions

1 Read and complete.

Use a *verb* to tell somebody what to do. Use ***Don't*** + *verb* to tell somebody what not to do.

Positive ✔	Negative ✘
Stand up.	1 Don't stand up.
2 ______ down.	Don't sit down.
Open your book.	3 ______ your book.

2 Look and write the instructions.

1 Sit on your chair.

2 ______ on the table.

3 ______ to your teacher.

4 ______ in your book.

5 ______ on the chairs.

6 ______ in the classroom.

3 Write two more classroom rules.

1 ✔ ______

2 ✘ ______

Grammar Review

1 Read and complete.

2 True or false? Write the correct sentences.

1 The books are on the floor. False. The books are on the shelf.

2 The bed is in the closet. ______

3 A bag is on the desk. ______

4 Some toys are on the bed. ______

5 The desk is under the bed. ______

3 Unscramble. Check (✔) the instructions from the story.

1 in. / Come — Come in. ✔

2 down. / Don't / sit ______ ☐

3 door. / Close / the ______ ☐

4 Don't / doors. / the / open ______ ☐

Grammar Challenge

1 Help Sharon find her things. Match and write.

1 Where are my books?

2 Is ________ your notebook?

3 Are ________ your crayons?

4 Where's my pencil case?

5 Stand up! Is ________ your blue notebook?

a Oh! Yes, it is. Thanks Mom!

b No, it isn't. My notebook is blue.

c They're on the chair.

d Yes, they are.

e It's in your bag. Look ________ the door.

2 Find a doll and an eraser. Write Sharon's questions and her mom's answers.

1 Where's my doll? ________ ________

2 ________ ________

It's My World!

What's in your bedroom? Where is it? Now talk to a friend.

Chapter 5

My Town

Lesson 1

1 Listen and number. Then say.

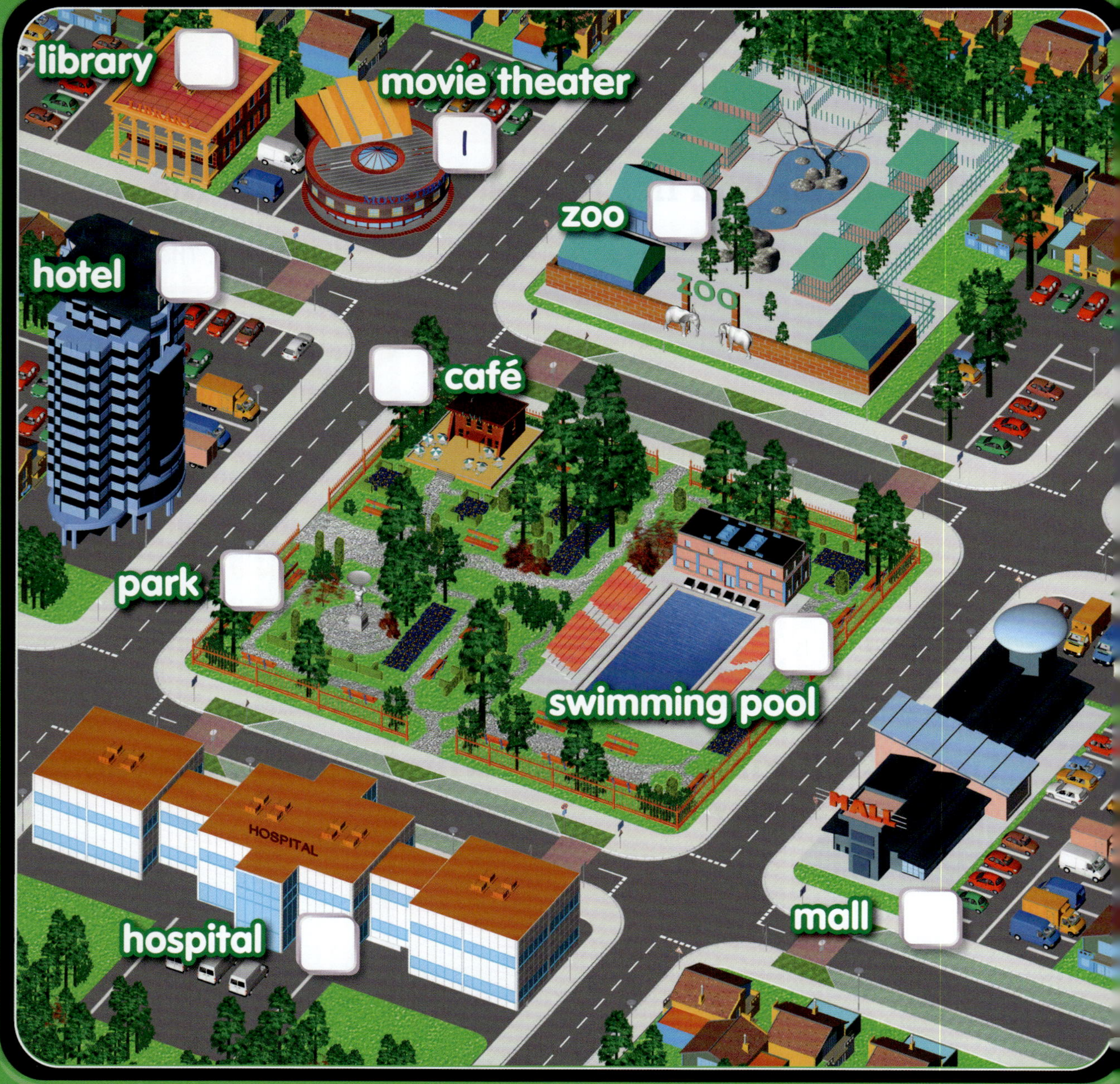

1 Look, count, and write.

movie theater	2	library		mall	
swimming pool		hotel			

2 Listen and circle T (true) or F (false).

1 There's a library. T / F

2 There are three malls. T / F

3 There isn't a swimming pool. T / F

4 There are two movie theaters. T / F

3 Ask and answer.

Is there a zoo?

No, there isn't.

How many hotels are there?

There are three.

Grammar Central

There's a zoo.
Is there a mall?
Yes, **there is**. / No, **there isn't**.
How many malls **are there**?
There are two.

Grammar Booster on page 74

Lesson 3 Tell Me a Story

1 Listen and read. Then act out.

2 Look at the story and think. What's it about?

3 Listen and read. What places are in the story?

a mall	☐	a movie theater	☐
a hospital	☐	a zoo	☐

Captain Navigate

Reader

Read the story in your Reader on pages 14–17.

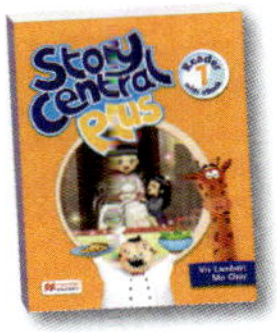

Lesson 4 Time to Think

1 Read the story in your Reader on pages 14–17 again.

2 Who is good? Who is bad? Write G (good) or B (bad).

3 Write. Ask Captain Navigate for help.

4 Talk about the story.

What other superheroes do you know?

Lesson 5

Song

1 Listen, count, and write. Then sing.

Beep, Beep, Beep!

There are cars and buses on the street.
Zoom! Vroom! Beep! Beep! Beep!
How many cars are there on the street?
How many buses? Zoom! Vroom! Beep!

There are trucks and taxis on the street.
Zoom! Vroom! Beep! Beep! Beep!
How many trucks are there on the street?
How many taxis? Zoom! Vroom! Beep!

There are vans and motorcycles on the street.
Zoom! Vroom! Beep! Beep! Beep!
How many vans are there on the street?
How many motorcycles? Zoom! Vroom! Beep!

2 Ask and answer.

How many buses are there?

There are two.

3 Listen and say the chant.

The bus goes beep, the van goes vroom.
Beep, beep, vroom, beep, beep, vroom.

Lesson 6

1 Listen and read.

2 Look at the story. Complete Libby's directions to Green Park.

1 Where's Green Park?

2 It's ......next to...... the zoo.

3 Take the ....

4 Go ....

5 Then, take the ....

Grammar Centre

Take the first left.
Go straight.
It's **across from** the mall.

Grammar Booster on page 75

1 Listen and read. Then write the number of the correct picture.

TRANSPORTATION

Bangkok is a big city in Thailand. There are a lot of houses, malls, and cafés. The streets in Bangkok are very busy. There are cars and motorcycles. There are buses and taxis. ☐ There are tuk-tuks, too. Tuk-tuks are blue and red. ☐ There's a long river in Bangkok called the Chao Phraya River. There are river buses ☐ on the Chao Phraya River.

2 Check (✔) the transportation in your town. Then talk to a friend.

In my town, there are buses and taxis.

taxis ☐ tuk-tuks ☐ river buses ☐ buses ☐

3 Class Vote!

Tuk-tuk or river bus?

Find Out More!

What other transportation is there? Search the Internet or ask your teacher.

Project

Lesson 8

Prepare

1 Make a town map and badges.

1

2

3

Showcase

2 Tell the story. Use your town map and badges.

1 Listen and write the numbers. Then answer.

library	1	mall		hospital	
hotel		café		park	

1 Is there a hospital? ....

2 Is there a zoo? ....

3 Is there a hotel? Yes, there are ....

4 How many cafés are there? ....

2 Look at the map. Complete the directions from the café to the swimming pool.

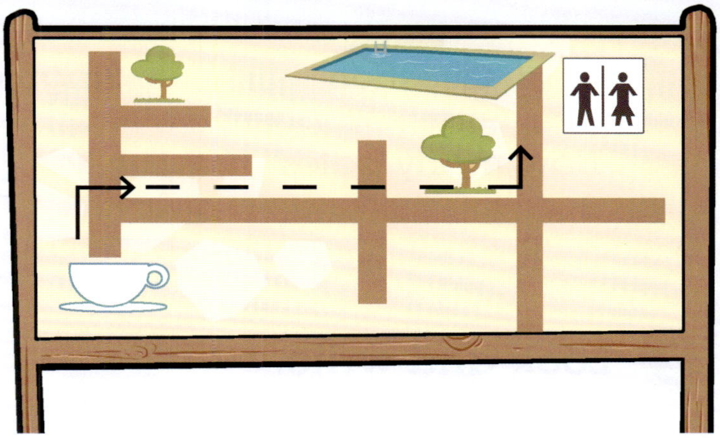

Go straight.

Take the ....

Then take the ....

It's ....

the bathroom.

3 Think about Chapter 5. Color the books.

Treasure Hunt!

Look back at pages 4 and 5. Find:

a red bus

Grammar Booster
There is and *There are*

1 Read and complete.

Use ***Is there ...?*** and ***Are there ...?*** to ask about things around us.

To answer, use ***There's / There isn't ...*** with singular nouns and ***There are / There aren't*** ... with plural nouns.

Question	Positive ✔	Negative ✘
1 Is there a mall?	Yes, there is.	No, there 2 ______.

Question	Singular (one)	Plural (more than one)
How many cafés 3 ______?	4 ______ a café.	5 ______ two cafés.

there**'s** = there is
there is**n't** = there is not

2 Look and write.

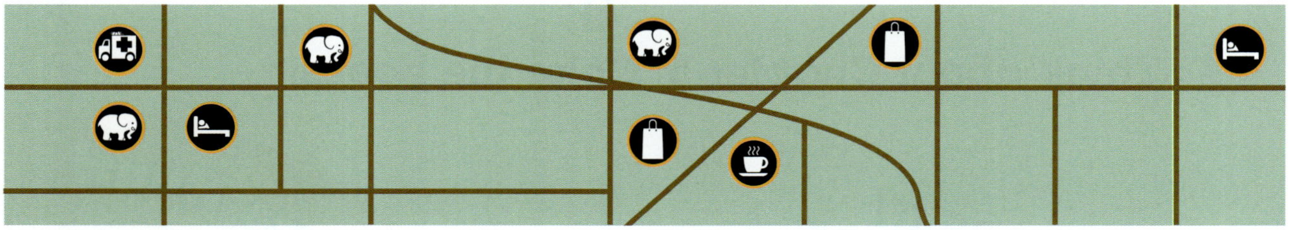

1 There's a hospital.

2 ______ two hotels.

3 ______ a café.

4 ______ three zoos.

5 **Q:** ______ school?

A: ______

6 **Q:** ______ malls are there?

A: ______ two malls.

Directions

1 Read and complete.

To give directions, use
Go straight and ***Take the first left / second right***.

Take the first
1 left.

2 ________
first right.

Take the
3 ________ left.

Go 4 ________.

To say where something is, use **It's next to / across from**.

It's 5 ________
to the movie
theater.

It's 6 ________
from the
movie theater.

2 Write the words in order. Then answer.

1 straight. / Go

Go straight.

2 first / the / left. / Take

____

3 right. / the / Take / first

____

4 zoo. / It's / the / across from

____

5 Where are you?

I'm at the ________________

Grammar Review

1 Read and circle.

2 Number the lines in order.

a Take the second right. The mall is across from the library ☐

b Excuse me. Is there a movie theater in this town? [1]

c Where's the mall? ☐

d Thanks! ☐

e Yes, there is. It's in the mall. ☐

3 Practice a new dialogue with a friend.

Is there a café in this town?

Yes, there is. It's …

Grammar Challenge

1 Read and circle.

My name's Anna and this is my house. 1 **There's** / **There are** three bedrooms. There's a kitchen and a living room. 2 **There's** / **There are** two bathrooms.

My house is in Townsville. It's a small town. There are a lot of houses. 3 **There isn't** / **There aren't** a hospital. There's a library 4 **across from** / **next to** the mall. 5 **There isn't** / **There aren't** a swimming pool. There's a big park. It's 6 **behind** / **next to** a hotel.

There are two hotels and two movie theaters in Townsville. One movie theater is 7 **across from** / **next to** a hotel. There's a movie theater 8 **across from** / **next to** my house, too.

9 **Where's** / **When's** your house? 10 **Is there** / **are there** a movie theater in your town?

2 Answer.

1 How many bedrooms are there in Anna's house? There are three bedrooms.

2 Where's the library? ....

3 Is there a swimming pool? ....

4 How many hotels are there? ....

5 Is there a hospital? ....

6 Where's the park? ....

It's My World!
Talk about your house and your town.

Chapter 6 My Family

Lesson 1

1 Listen and number. Then say.

mom	1	grandma		brother		aunt	
grandpa		uncle		dad		sister	

1 Listen and read. Then check (✔) the correct picture.

I have a mom and a dad.	My grandpa is tall.
I don't have a brother.	I have two grandmas.
I have two sisters.	I don't have any aunts or uncles.

2 Point to the pictures. Ask and answer.

My mom is tall.

I have .... brothers.

I .... have a grandpa.

I .... a grandma.

3 Talk to a friend about your family.

I have three sisters and one brother.

Grammar Central

I have two sisters.

I don't have a brother.

I don't have any brothers or sisters

Grammar Booster on page 88

Lesson 3 Tell Me a Story

1 Listen and read. Then act out.

2 Look at the story and think. What's it about?

3 Listen and read. Who is in the story?

dad ☐ sister ☐ uncle ☐

Reader Read the story in your Reader on pages 18–20.

Lesson 4 Time to Think

1 Read the story in your Reader on pages 18–20 again.

I Can Read!
Look at picture 13 in your Reader. Why is 'HOORAY!' in capitals?

2 Complete the blanks.

I have ______________ brothers.
I have ______________ sister.

3 Who helps you? Say thank you.

THANK YOU

To ______________________________

Thank you for
- ☐ my present.
- ☐ helping me with my homework.
- ☐ being my friend.

From ______________________________

4 Talk about the story.

Do you know any stories about families?

Lesson 5

Song

1 Listen and number. Then sing.

My Pets

I have a turtle [2] and a cat. [ ]
I have a hamster [ ] and a rat. [ ]
I have a fish [ ] and a mouse. [ ]
They all live here in my house.

I love my pets, and they love me.
I love my pets. They're my family.
I don't have any brothers or sisters, you see.
My pets are my family!

I have a bird [ ] and a dog. [ ]
I have a rabbit [ ] and a frog. [ ]
All these animals live with me.
My pets are my family!

2 Play a chain game.

I have a bird.

I have a bird and a dog.

I have a bird and a dog and a frog.

3 Listen and say the chant.

I have a hamster in my house.
A hungry hamster in my house.

Lesson 6

1 Listen and read.

I have a lot of friends!

2 Look at the picture below. Complete the blanks for Tom.

1 Do you have any .... brothers, Tom?

2 ....

3 Their .... Jack and Bobby.

Grammar Centr

Do you have any brothers or sisters?
Yes, **I do**. / No, **I dor**
Their names are Lisc and Laura.

Grammar Booster on page 89

1 Listen and read.

What Animals Need

Before

Do you have a house with a big yard?
Do you love animals?

Buddy is hungry.
Please help.

Give Buddy a warm bed and a home.

After

Now I have a big yard to play in.

I have food and water.

I have a warm bed and a big family.
I love my family!

2 Check (✔) the things that animals need.

food	✔	a bike	☐	a bed	☐
water	☐	a home	☐	a TV	☐

3 Class survey. Ask and answer.

4 Class Vote!

Cats or dogs?

Find Out More!

Choose another animal. Find out what they need. Search the Internet or ask your teacher.

Project

Lesson 8

Prepare

1 Make a funny family.

Showcase

2 Tell the story. Use your funny family.

1 Listen and match.

1

2

3

Jake ☐ Emily ☐ Brad ☐

2 Look and complete the blanks.

Boy: Do you have ...... any ...... pets?

Girl: Yes, I .... I have a ....

and a dog. Their .... are Kitty

and Lucky. I .... two hamsters.

.... names .... Harry and Henry.

3 Think about Chapter 6. Color the books.

Treasure Hunt!

Look back at pages 4 and 5. Find:

a rabbit

Grammar Booster

Have and don't have

1 Read and complete.

Use ***I have ...*** and ***I don't have (any) ...*** to talk about your family.

Positive ✔	**Negative** ✘
1 I have a brother.	2 ______ a sister.
3 ______ two sisters.	I don't have 4 ______ aunts or uncles.

2 Look and write.

My name's Nadia and this is my family.

1 I have a grandma and a grandpa.

2 I ______ a mom and a dad.

3 I have one ______ and three ______.

4 I ______ a cat.

5 I ______ any aunts ______ uncles.

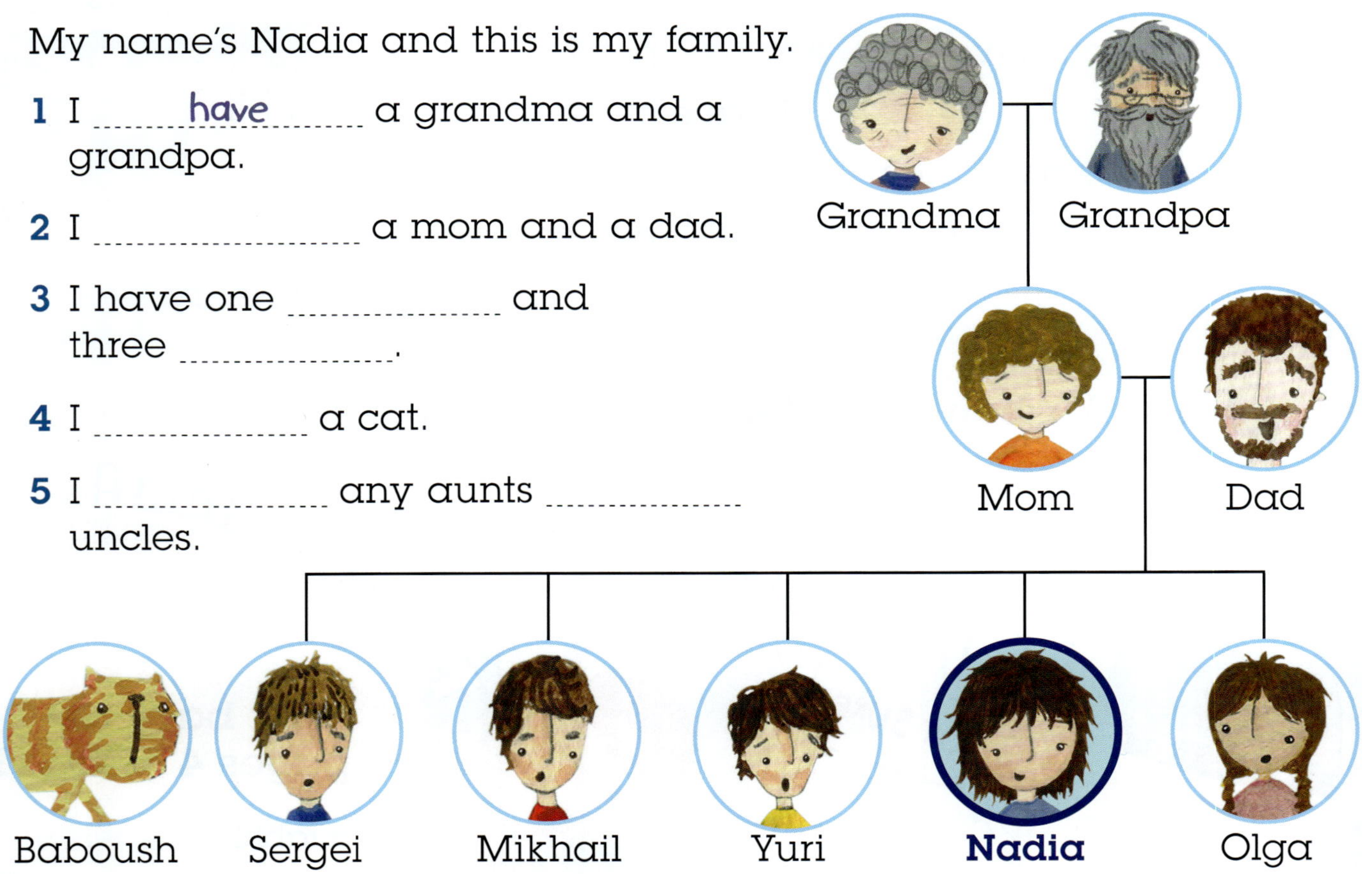

Do you have any ...?

1 Read and complete.

Use ***Do you have any ...?*** or ***How many ... do you have?*** to ask about family and pets.

Question	Positive ✔	Negative ✘
How many pets **1** do you have ?	I have two cats. **2** ________ names are Sam and Pat.	I don't have any dogs.
Do you have **3** ________ brothers or sisters?	Yes, I **4** ________. Their names are Mike and Jane.	No, I **5** ________.

2 Look, then write Uma's answers.

1 Do you have any brothers? — Yes, I do.

2 What are their names? — ________ Henry and Al.

3 Do you have any sisters? — No, ________.

4 How many pets do you have? — ________ two pets.

5 What are their names? — ________ Pip and Trixie.

Name: Uma

Age: 8 years old

Brothers: 2 (Henry and Al)

Sisters: None

Pets: 2 (Pip and Trixie)

Grammar Review

1 Read and complete.

2 Match and complete the dialogue.

1 How many grandmas do you have? — b

2 How many grandpas ______________?

3 Do you have ______ aunts or uncles?

4 ______________ people are there in your family?

a I have two aunts, but I ______________ any uncles.

b I have two grandmas.

c There are eight!

d I have one grandpa.

Grammar Challenge

b

a

c

d

1 Read and number the family photos.

1 I'm **Sammy**. I have a brother and a sister. I have three dogs and a hamster. I don't have a big yard, but my house is across from the park. b

2 I'm **Alex**. I have a brother and two sisters. I have two dogs and a cat. Do you have any pets?

3 My name's **Taylor**. I have two brothers and one sister. I don't have a dog or a hamster. My favorite toy is my teddy bear. It's cute.

2 Now write about the other family in Activity 1.

My name's **Teri**.

It's My World!

Talk about your family, your pets, and your toys.

Chapter 7 Strange Creatures

Lesson 1

1 Listen, read, and number. Then say.

1 Listen, read, and number.

My monster has three legs and a short tail. It has a long neck. ☐

My monster is brown. It has a big head and a small body. It has two long arms. ☐

My monster is small and black. It has four small hands. It doesn't have any legs. ☐

2 Look at the other monster. Circle the correct description.

1 It has a (big) / small head.

2 It has two / doesn't have any arms.

3 It has two / doesn't have any legs.

4 It has two / four hands.

Grammar Central

It has a big head.
It has four legs.
It doesn't have any arms.

Grammar Booster on page 102

Lesson 3

1 Listen and read. Then act out.

2 Look at the story and think. What's it about?

3 Listen and read. What does Doodle have?

short legs ☐ big feet ☐ long arms ☐

Good Friends

Reader Read the story in your Reader on pages 21–24.

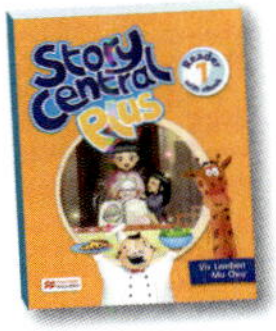

Lesson 4 Time to Think

1 Read the story in your Reader on pages 21–24 again.

I Can Read!

When do we use these? **!**

2 Check (✓) Doodle's mom.

 ☐

 ☐

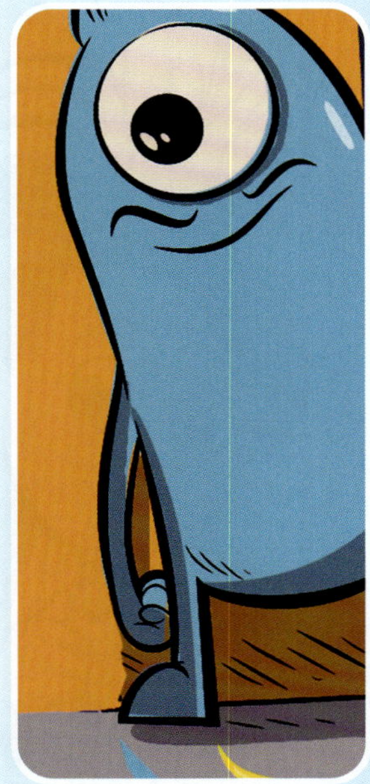 ☐

3 Who are your good friends?

My good friends are ....

4 Talk about the story.

Lesson 5

Song

1 **Listen and check (✔) the correct alien. Then sing.**

I'm an Alien

I have one big eye,
I don't have a nose,
I have three big ears,
And six little toes.

I have long green hair,
On my big head.
I have a small mouth,
My mouth is red.

I'm an alien. I'm a small, green alien.
I have one big eye on my face!
I'm an alien. I'm a small, green alien.
I come from Outer Space!

2 **Play a guessing game.**

How many eyes does it have?

It has six eyes. It doesn't have a mouth.

Number 3 is your alien!

3 **Listen and say the chant.**

The moon has a face. A face in space.
That face in space is the moon.

Lesson 6

1 Listen and read.

2 Complete the description of Biblio.

1 He has ____two____ eyes.

2 He ________________ any ears.

3 He ________________ any legs.

4 How many arms does he have?

________________________________.

Grammar Central

She has two eyes.
How many legs **does she have**?
She doesn't have any legs.

Grammar Booster on page 103

1 Listen and read. Then number.

The Planets

The Sun is a big star in space. There are eight planets. They go around the Sun in a big circle. Mercury is next to the Sun. Then Venus is next to Mercury.

Our planet is called Earth. Earth is the third planet from the sun. It has one moon. Next to Earth is Mars. Mars has two moons. Next to Mars is Jupiter. Jupiter is big and red. Saturn is next to Jupiter. Saturn has rings. Then, there is Uranus, and then Neptune.

☐ Earth ☐ Neptune ☐ Jupiter ☐ Saturn ☐ Mars ☐ Mercury ☐ Venus ☐ Uranus

2 **Class Vote!**

Are there any aliens in space? Yes or no?

Find Out More!

Find more facts about the planets. Search the Internet or ask your teacher.

Project

Lesson 8

Prepare

1 Make an alien.

Showcase

2 Tell the story. Use your aliens.

1 Listen and check (✔) the correct monster.

2 Write T (Tom) or B (Biblio).

1 He has two legs. T
2 He has long arms. B
3 He has two ears. ....
4 He doesn't have a nose. ....
5 He doesn't have any feet. ....

3 Think about Chapter 7. Color the books.

Treasure Hunt!

Look back at pages 4 and 5. Find:

a long tail

Grammar Booster

Has and doesn't have

1 Read and complete.

Use ***It has*** **...** and ***It doesn't have*** **...** to talk about animals' bodies.

Positive ✔	**Negative** ✘
It **1** has a long neck.	It **2** ______ have a big head.
It **3** ______ four legs.	It doesn't **4** ______ any arms.

2 Write sentences. Then draw the alien.

1 This alien / big head ✔ This alien has a big head.

2 It / short neck ✔ ______ a short neck.

3 It / long body ✔ ______ a long body.

4 It / arms ✘ ______ any arms.

5 It / four legs ✔ ______

6 It / tail ✘ ______

Does he / she have ...?

1 Read and complete.

Use ***How many ... does he / she / it have?*** or ***Does he / she / it have ...?*** to ask about a person or animal's face or body.

Question	Positive ✔	Negative ✘
1 How many arms **2** ______ it have?	It **3** ______ three arms.	It **4** ______ any arms.
5 ______ he have long legs?	Yes, he does.	No, he **6** ______.

2 Read, complete, and find the correct doll.

Does she have long hair?

Yes, she **1** does.

Does she have green eyes?

No, she **2** ______.

How **3** ______ arms does she have?

She has two arms.

Her name is **4** ______.

1 Poppy
2 Polly
3 Tilly
4 Billie

3 Choose a different doll. Ask and answer with a friend.

Does she have long legs?

Grammar Review

1 Read, choose, and complete.

Does it | doesn't have | ~~How many~~ | it does | It doesn't | It has

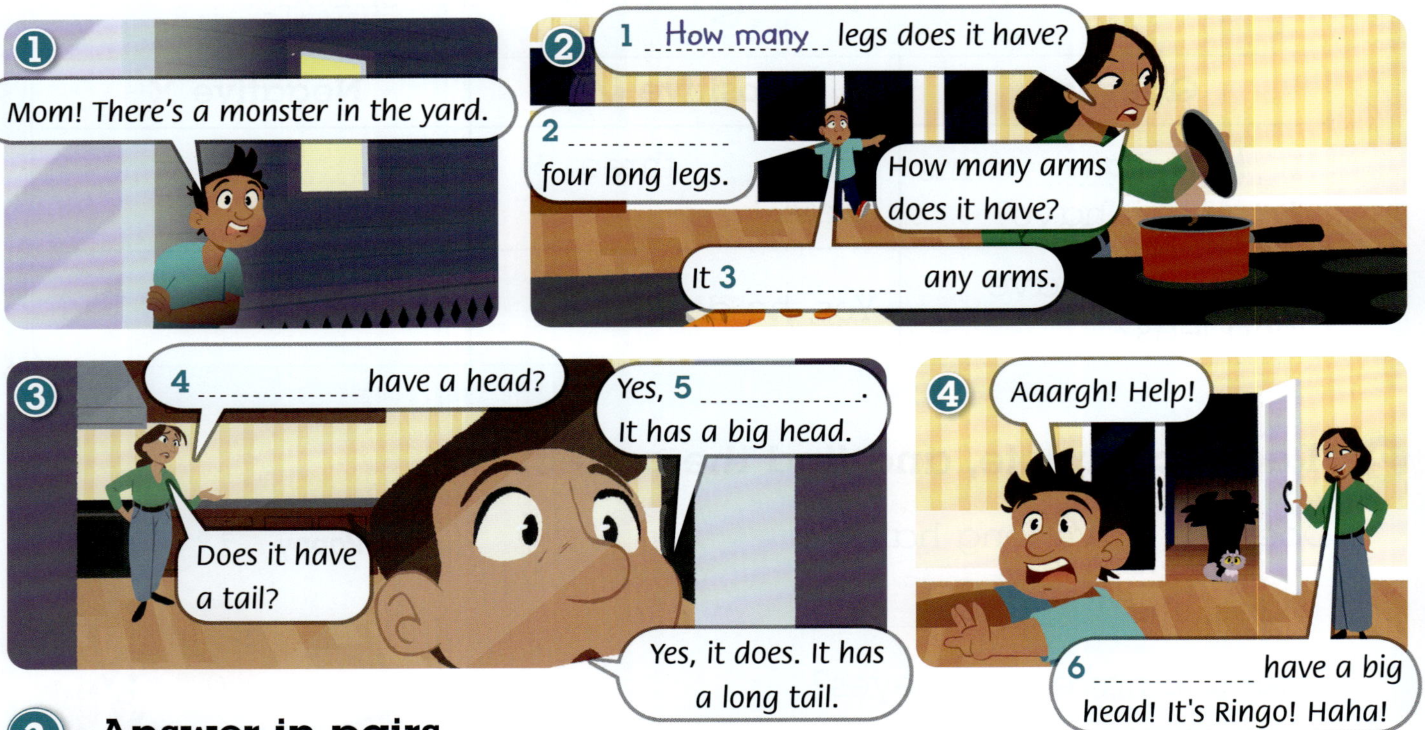

2 Answer in pairs.

How many legs does it have?

Does it have big teeth?

Is it a lion?

What is it?

How many legs does it have?

Does it have a long tail?

Is it a monster?

What is it?

1 Read and match. Draw lines.

I have brown hair and blue eyes. I have a black and white cat. I have two brothers. I don't have a sister.

I have long hair and brown eyes. I have a cat and a hamster. Their names are Tick & Tock. I have two sisters.

I have short, blonde hair and glasses. I have a hamster. My apartment is next to the park.

Derry  Mary  Jake  Sara 

1  2  3  4 

a  b  c  d 

2 Answer the questions in pairs.

1 Does Jake have brown hair? Yes, he does.

2 How many pets does he have? ____________

3 Does it have a long tail? ____________

4 Does he have any brothers or sisters? ____________

5 Does he have a house or an apartment? ____________

It's My World!

Describe a classmate for a friend to guess.

Chapter 8 I Like Food!

Lesson 1

1 Listen and number. Then say.

Lesson 2

1 Listen, read, and match.

1

I like chicken and pasta. I like broccoli, but I don't like peas.

2

I like pizza, but I don't like pasta. I like salad.

3

I like burgers and fries. I like peas, but I don't like salad.

2 Listen and check (✔) (I like …) or cross (✘) (I don't like …) for Ana.

	Salad	Broccoli	Chicken	Fish	Fries	Peas	Pasta	Pizza
Ana	✔							
Me								

3 Now complete the chart for you.

4 Talk to a friend.

I like salad, but I don't like broccoli.

Grammar Central

I like pizza.
I don't like broccoli.
I like pizza, but **I don't like** broccoli.

Grammar Booster on page 116

Lesson 3 Tell Me a Story

1 Listen and read. Then act out.

2 Look at the story and think. Where are they?

3 Listen and read. What food is in the story?

pizza ☐ fish ☐ salad ☐

I LIKE CAKE!

Reader

Read the story in your Reader on pages 25–27.

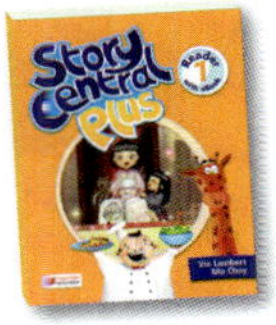

Lesson 4 Time to Think

1 Read the story in your Reader on pages 25–27 again.

I Can Read!

What are these?

“ ”

2 Why is Chip unhappy?

---

3 Draw food that makes you happy.

4 Talk about the story.

Lesson 5

Song

1 Listen and match. Then sing.

Ice Cream and Cake

On Monday, I have salad.
On Tuesday, I have cheese.
On Wednesday, I have chicken.
More chicken, please!

On Thursday, I have pasta.
On Friday, I have rice.
Saturday, is pizza night.
Mmm! Pizza's very nice!

Sunday, is my favorite day.
You'll love the food I make!
For a special treat,
I have ice cream and cake!

2 Write about your food. Then talk with a friend.

On Monday I have pizza.

3 Listen and say the chant.

Chicken and cheese, chicken and cheese,
More chicken and cheese, but no fish, please!

Lesson 6

1 Listen and read.

2 Complete the blanks for Ellie.

1 Do you like .... pizza?

2 ....

3 .... chicken?

4 ....

Grammar Central

Do you like pizza?

Yes, **I do.** / No, **I don't**

Grammar Booster on page 117

1 Listen and read.

Lunchtime

Tuesday, June 1st

This is my lunch today. There's cheese pizza with salad. Pizza is ok, but not every day. I like salad. It's good for you. There's ice cream, too. I like ice cream, but it's not very healthy!

★★★

Wednesday, June 2nd

Ugh! A terrible lunch today. Burger and fries. No vegetables! I don't like burgers and fries. They aren't healthy.

★

Thursday, June 3rd

Lunch today is chicken, rice, broccoli, and fruit. Very healthy! I like rice, and I love chicken. Fruit is OK.

★★★★★

What do you think? Which lunch do you like? What do you have for lunch? Show me your pictures!

2 Write the food words in the correct places.

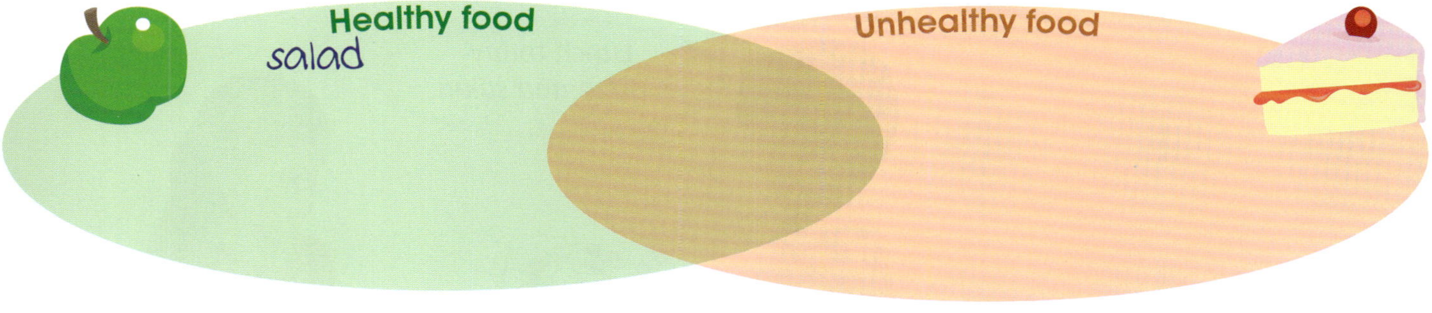

3 Class Vote!

Ice cream or fruit?

Find Out More!

Find three more healthy foods.
Search the Internet or ask your teacher.

Project

Lesson 8

Prepare

1 Make different food.

Showcase

2 Tell the story. Use your food.

1 Listen and check (✔) (I like…) or cross (✘) (I don't like…).

2 Write answers for you.

1 Do you like cake? ....

2 Do you like cheese? ....

3 Do you like ice cream? ....

4 Do you like fish? ....

5 Do you like rice? ....

3 Think about Chapter 8. Color the books.

Treasure Hunt!

Look back at pages 4 and 5. Find:

Monday

Grammar Booster

Like and don't like

1 Read and complete.

Use ***I like ...*** or ***I don't like ...*** to talk about things you like or don't like.

Positive ✔	**Negative ✘**
I **1** like pizza.	I **2** ______ like green beans.
Positive ✔ + *and* + positive ✔	**Positive ✔ + *but* + Negative ✘**
I **3** ______ chicken and I like peas.	I **4** ______ chicken, but I don't **5** ______ salad.
I like pasta **6** ______ I like broccoli.	I don't like broccoli, **7** ______ I like fish.

2 Look and write.

1 I like pizza.

2 ______ peas.

3 ______ broccoli, but ______ chicken.

4 ______ pizza and ______ pasta.

5 ______ and ______.

6 ______, but ______.

☺	☹
pizza	burgers
salad	green beans
pasta	peas
broccoli	chicken

Do you like ...?

1 Read and complete.

Use ***Do you like ...?*** to ask what somebody likes.

Question	Answer ✔ ✘
1 Do you like pizza?	Yes, I 2 ....
3 .... ice cream?	No, I 4 ....

2 Complete the questions. Then write answers for you.

1 **Q:** Do you like hamsters?

A: ....

2 **Q:** .... broccoli?

A: ....

3 **Q:** .... cats?

A: ....

4 **Q:** .... peas?

A: ....

3 Write two sentences about you.

1 I like ...., but ....

2 I like .... and ....

Grammar Review

1 Read and circle.

2 Read and complete.

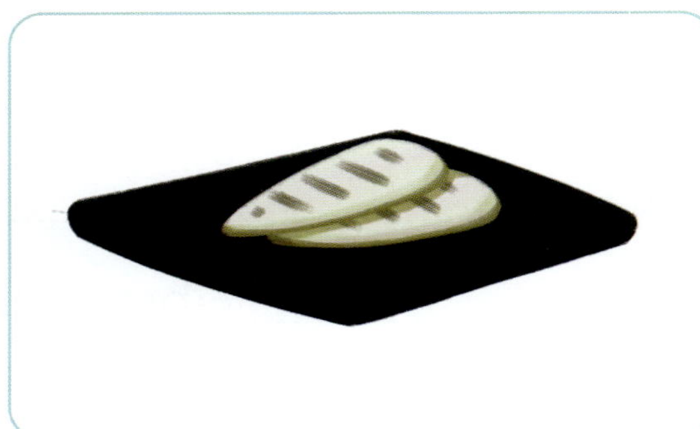

1 I ___don't___ like rice.

This isn't rice. ________ ice cream.

Oh, good! I ________ ice cream!

2 I ________ fish.

This ________ fish. It's chicken.

Oh, good! ________________!

Grammar Challenge

1 Read and find.

Do you like ...

	cats?	dogs?	salad?	fish?	bikes?	robots?
Jess	☺	☹	☺	☹	☺	☹
Ciara	☺	☹	☺	☺	☺	☹
Dennis	☺	☺	☺	☹	☺	☺

1 I like cats and dogs. I have a dog, but I don't have a cat. I like salad, but I don't like fish. I like robots and bikes. **Who am I?** ________

2 I have two cats. I like cats, but I don't like dogs. I don't like fish, but my favorite food is salad. I don't like robots, but I like bikes. I have a blue bike. **Who am I?** ________

2 Write about Ciara.

I **1** _don't like_ dogs, but I **2** ________ cats. I **3** ________ two cats; their names **4** ________ Patty and Sue. I **5** ________ fish and I **6** ________ salad. My **7** ________________ toy is my bike. I **8** ____________ robots.

3 Ask and answer with a partner.

Do you like cats?

It's My World!

What's for lunch today? Do you like it?

Chapter 9 Sports and Music

Lesson 1

1 Listen and number. Then say.

Get in Shape!

ride a bike

1

run

swim

dance

skate

play soccer

1 

2 

3 

4 

5 

6 

1 Look, listen, and circle.

1 It can / can't swim.
2 It can / can't run.
3 It can / can't ride a bike.
4 It can / can't skate.

2 Listen and check (✔) (Yes, I can.) or cross (✘) (No, I can't.) for Uma and Fred.

Can you ...	Uma	Fred	Me
ride a bike?	✔		
swim?			
play soccer?			
dance?			
skate?			
run?			

3 Now complete the chart for you.

4 Talk to a friend.

I can run, but I can't swim.

Grammar Central

He can run.
He can't skate.
Can you ride a bike?
Yes, **I can.**/No, **I can't.**

Grammar Booster on page 130

Lesson 3

1 Listen and read. Then act out.

2 Look at the story and think. What's it about?

3 Listen and read. What items are in the story?

fish ☐ cat ☐ violin ☐

The Magic Violin

Reader Read the story in your Reader on pages 28–31.

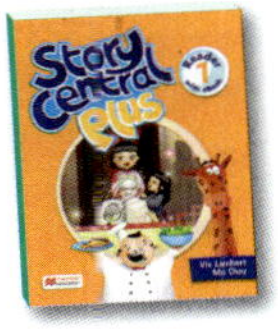

Lesson 4 Time to Think

1. Read the story in your Reader on pages 28–31 again.

I Can Read!

Is this story better read out loud?

Which words rhyme?

2. **Check (✓) what the fish can do in the story.**

fly ☐ sing ☐ dance ☐

3. **Write another verse. Then draw.**

Look at those ....

Those .... can ....!

.... can't ....

Don't be silly, Tim.

Oh, yes, they can,

When I play my violin.

4. **Talk about the story.**

Do you know another rhyming story?

Lesson 5

Song

1 Listen and number. Then sing.

Let's Play Together

Can you play the piano, piano, piano? 2
Can you play the piano?
Yes, I can.

Can you play the drums, drums, drums? ☐
Can you play the drums?
Yes, I can.

Can you play the guitar …? ☐

Can you play the tambourine …? ☐

Can you play the recorder …? ☐

Can you play the violin …? ☐

Let's all play together, together, together
Let's all play together.
Yes, we can!

2 Ask and answer.

Can you play the piano?

No, I can't.

3 Listen and say the chant.

Bang! Bang! Bang! Drum. Drum. Drum.
Bang, bang, bang on the drum, drum, drum!

Lesson 6

1 Listen and read.

Story Central Has Talent!

2 Complete the blanks for Tom and Ellie.

1 Tom can *play the guitar*.
2 He can't ______.
3 ______ he sing? ______.
4 Ellie ______ sing.
5 She ______ play the piano.

Grammar Central

Can she sing?
Yes, **she can**. /
No, **she can't**.

Grammar Booster on page 131

1 Listen and read.

World Instruments

This instrument is from Australia. It's a **didgeridoo**. It's very long. It comes from a tree. You play the didgeridoo with your mouth. Native Australian people sing and dance to the sound of the didgeridoo.

This instrument is from Tibet. It's a **Tibetan hand bell**. It's very small. Tibetan hand bells can be used in meditation. People in Tibet play the hand bell with their left hand.

This instrument is from Hawaii. You play it with your nose! It's called a **Hawaiian nose flute**. It's long and thin.

Ccn you play any musical instruments? Do you use your mouth, hands, or nose?

2 Circle T (true) or F (false).

1 The didgeridoo is from Australia. T / F
2 You play the didgeridoo with your nose. T / F
3 The Tibetan hand bell is very small. T / F
4 You play the Tibetan hand bell with your right hand. T / F
5 The Hawaiian nose flute is from Europe. T / F

3 Class Vote!

Play or listen to music?

Find Out More!

Find out about another unusual instrument from around the world. What parts of the body do you use to play it?

Project

Lesson 8

Prepare

1 **Make an instrument.**

Showcase

2 **Tell the story. Use your instruments.**

1 Listen and check (✔) (Yes, he can.) or cross (✘) (No, he can't.). Then write answers.

swim ✔ skate ☐ dance ☐
ride a bike ☐ play soccer ☐

1 Can he swim? Yes, he can.
2 Can he ride a bike? ....
3 Can he skate? ....
4 Can he dance? ....
5 Can he play soccer? ....

2 Write answers for you.

1 Can you skate? ....
2 Can you play the guitar? ....
3 Can you ride a bike? ....
4 Can you swim? ....

3 Think about Chapter 9. Color the books.

Treasure Hunt!

Look back at pages 4 and 5. Find:

skates

Grammar Booster

Can and can't

1 Read and complete.

Use ***can*** / ***can't*** + *verb* to talk about abilities.

Positive ✔	**Negative** ✘
I **1** can run. He **3** ______ ride a bike.	I **2** ______ skate. She **4** ______ dance.
Question	**Short answer** ✔ ✘
Can you swim?	Yes, I **5** ______. No, I **6** ______.

2 Look and write.

1 Can you swim? Yes, I can.

2 ______ skate? ______

3 ______ play soccer? ______

4 ______ dance? ______

3 Write about the girl in Activity 2.

1 She can swim and she can play soccer.

2 She can swim, but ______.

3 ______, but ______.

Can she ...?

1 Read and complete.

Use ***Can he / she / it*** + *verb*? to ask about somebody's abilities.

Question	Answer ✔
1 ___Can___ he swim?	Yes, he 2 ________.
3 ________ she play the piano?	No, she 4 ________.

2 Look. Write the questions or the answers.

John 	✔	✘	✔	✘
Ana 	✘	✔	✘	✔

1 Can John play the guitar? ___Yes, he can.___

2 Can he play the recorder? ________________

3 Can Ana sing? ________________

4 Can Ana skate? ________________

5 ________________ No, he can't.

6 ________________ Yes, she can.

Grammar Review

1 **Read, choose, and complete.**

Can he swim	~~Can you walk~~	can eat
can't walk	No, he can't	No, I can't

2 **Read and write *can* or *can't*.**

Grammar Challenge

My name's Greta. I have a mom and a dad, a brother, and a sister. My family can play a lot of instruments. We are in a band called Super Six! My dad can play the piano. He's tall and he has big hands. My mom can play the guitar, but she can't play the piano. My brother can play the drums and my sister can play the recorder. I can sing and I can dance. There are five people in my family. Why is the band named Super Six? Because my dog Benji can play the tambourine with his mouth!

1 Read and match.

1 Greta has	a big hands.
2 Her dad has	b play the piano.
3 Her mom can't	c play the tambourine.
4 Greta can sing	d a brother and a sister.
5 Benji can	e and she can dance.

2 Make a band. Talk to your friends. Who can play an instrument? Who can sing? Think of a name for your band. Then write.

Our band is named ______________________.

There are ______ people in our band.

I can ______________________________

____

It's My World!
What instruments do you know? How many can you say in English?

YLE words ✔ in **BOLD**

Word List

Macmillan Education Limited
4 Crinan Street
London N1 9XW

Companies and representatives throughout the world

Story Central Plus Level 1 Student Book ISBN 978-1-380-05913-0
Story Central Plus Level 1 Student Book with Student eBook and Reader and CLIL eBook ISBN 978-1-380-06083-9
Story Central Plus Level 1 Student Book with Reader, CLIL Book, Student eBook, Reader eBook, and CLIL eBook (Brazil)
ISBN: 978-1-380-06082-2

This edition published 2021
First edition entitled "Story Central" published 2015 by Macmillan Education Limited

Designed by Liz Adcock and Pronk Media, Inc.
Illustrated by Aardvart pp. 93, 120b; Ilias Arahovitis (Beehive Illustration) p. 106; Valentina Belloni (MB Artists) pp. 122–123, 125; Robin Boyden (Pickled Ink) pp. 94–95, 96, 97; Paco Cavero (Sylvie Poggio Artist Agency) pp. 17, 31t, 59, 73, 87, 101t, 101, 129; Inna Chernyak (Plum Pudding) pp. 38–39, 40, 41t; Marcus Cutler (Sylvie Poggio Artist Agency) pp. 108–109, 110, 111; Anna Hancock (Beehive Illustration) pp. 11rm, 13b, 23, 25r, 27b, 29b, 37, 39r, 42b, 44m, 51t, 53r, 55b, 65, 67r, 69b, 79, 81r, 83b, 95r, 97b, 109r, 122, 123r, 125b; Beth Hughes (The Bright Agency) pp 18, 19, 20, 21, 46, 47, 48, 49, 74, 75, 76, 102, 103, 104, 105, 130, 131, 132, 133; Ellie Jenkins (Advocate Art) pp. 80–81, 82, 83; Ayesha Lopez (Advocate Art) pp. 52–53, 54, 55; Louise Redshaw (Plum Pudding) pp. 24–25, 26, 27; Laszlo Veres (Beehive Illustration) pp. 8, 50, 64, 92; Dan Widdowson (The Bright Agency) pp 32, 33, 34, 35, 60, 61, 62, 63, 88, 89, 90, 91, 117, 118; Steven Wood (Advocate Art) pp 4-129 (border design and main character artwork) 4–5, 6–7, 10, 14, 24l, 28, 31m, 38l, 42, 52l, 56, 66l, 70, 80l, 84, 94l, 98, 108l, 112, 122l, 126; Patricia Yuste (Advocate Art) pp10, 11, 12, 13.
Cover design by Wild Apple Design Ltd. and Roberto Martinez
Cover illustration Steven Wood (Advocate Art)
Picture research by Composure

Author's acknowledgements
Thank you to everyone at Macmillan for their support and for allowing us to work in 'our way'. For patience and tolerance of late-night working, thank you to our families.

The authors and publishers would like to thank the following for permission to reproduce their photographs:

Alamy Stock Photo/Andrew Twort (ccr)p. 106, Alamy Stock Photo/Arco Images GmbH (tc)p. 43, Alamy Stock Photo/blickwinkel (br)

Printed and bound in Brazil.
2025
10

p. 36, Alamy Stock Photo/Canva Pty Ltd (cr)p Photo/Christopher Bradshaw (a)p. 22, Alamy S Hoare (cr)p. 113, Alamy Stock Photo/Edwin Re 127, Alamy Stock Photo/Emily Lai (cr)p. 15, Ala Eureka (bl)p. 36, Alamy Stock Photo/Golden Pixe Alamy Stock Photo/Iain Stuart MacGregor (tcl)p. 1 Photo/Image Professionals GmbH (ccl)p. 106, (ccr)p. Stock Photo/imageBROKER (tl)p. 120, Alamy Stock P Bildarchiv GmbH (tl)p. 12, (tr)p. 85, Alamy Stock Photo/ (2)p. 36, Alamy Stock Photo/Life on white (bc)p. 36, (bcr) p. 36, Alamy Stock Photo/Matthew Rex (4)p. 45, Alamy St neal and molly jansen (ccl)p. 113, Alamy Stock Photo/Osca (6)p. 36, Alamy Stock Photo/Paul Bradforth (tcr)p. 106, Alamy Photo/Simon Reddy (3)p. 71, Alamy Stock Photo/Stocktrek Ima Inc. (cc)p. 99, Alamy Stock Photo/Tim Gainey (tr)p. 15, Alamy S Photo/toy Alan King (d)p. 22, Alamy Stock Photo/vanillaechoes (b p. 106, Alamy Stock Photo/VeterinaryImages (tl)p. 85, Alamy Stock Photo/Viktor Fischer (tl)p. 106, Alamy Stock Photo/wacpan (tcl) p. 15; **Getty Images**/Chris Upton (cr)p. 43, Getty Images/Isu (tr) p. 12,Getty Images/jangeltun (cc)p. 119, Getty Images/Jose Luis Pelaez Inc (cc)p. 107, Getty Images/Jules Frazier (bl)p. 113, Getty Images/Londolozi Images/Mint Images (tr)p. 43, Getty Images/ Manoj Shah (tl)p. 45, Getty Images/Massimo Mei (tcr)p. 43, Getty Images/Peter Dazeley (tl)p. 29, Getty Images/photoman73 (cc)p. 120, Getty Images/roevin (1)p. 71, Getty Images/spfoto (cl)p. 107, Getty Images/Stefan Auth (tc)p. 12, Getty Images/Stephen Frink (2) p. 45, Getty Images/Stockbyte (cl)p. 15, Getty Images/stockstudioX (3)p. 45, Getty Images/tacar (background) p. 113, Getty Images/ Tomas Rodriguez (cc)p. 36, Getty Images/Travelpix Ltd (cc)p. 15, Getty Images/Winfried Wisniewski (3)p. 36, Getty Images/Zocha_K (1)p. 36; **Macmillan Education Limited**/59122 (tr)p. 106, Macmillan Education Limited/BRAND X (bcl)p. 113, Macmillan Education Limited/David Lee/Alamy Stock Photo (ccr)p. 113, Macmillan Education Limited/DIGITAL VISION (tcl)p. 29, Macmillan Education Limited/GeoffBlack,Geoff Black (c)p. 22, Macmillan Education Limited/GETTY (tc)p. 15, (tr)p. 36, (bl)p. 106, Macmillan Education Limited/ImageSource (br)p. 106, Macmillan Education Limited/ Lisa Payne (bcl)p. 106, Macmillan Education Limited/MACMILLAN AUSTRALIA (tcr)p. 29, Macmillan Education Limited/NordicImages/ Alamy Stock Photo (e)p. 22, Macmillan Education Limited/Paul Bricknell (b)p. 22, (f)p. 22, Macmillan Education Limited/PhotoDisc/ Getty Images (cl)p. 113, Macmillan Education Limited/Stockbyte Royalty Free Photos (tr)p. 29; **Shutterstock**/fizkes (tr)p. 78, Shutterstock/Manny DaCunha (tc)p. 120, Shutterstock/Samuel Micut (tr)p. 120, Shutterstock/sduraku (cl)p. 127; **Superstock**/ (cc)p 78, Superstock/Blend Images/Blend Images (cr)p. 120, Superstock/ Design Pics/Design Pics (cr)p. 57, Superstock/Jon Bower (tr)p. 57, Superstock/Otto Stadler/imageBROKER/imageBROKER (2)p. 71, Superstock/Salva Garrigues/ age fotostock (cc)p. 127.

Commissioned photography by MMStudios pp. 9, 16, 23, 30, 44, 51 58, 72, 85, 86, 100, 114, 128.

Prop artwork by Carla Drury

We would like to thank the following for their help with the photos in the book: Charlie, Charlotte, Jasmine, Lewis, Rafferty and Tiharna.

Story Central Plus

Activity Book 1
with Digital Book

macmillan education

Viv Lambert

Macmillan Education Limited
4 Crinan Street
London N1 9XW

Companies and representatives throughout the world

Story Central Plus Level 1 Activity Book ISBN 978-1-380-06013-6
Story Central Plus Level 1 Activity Book with Digital Activity Book 978-1-380-06992-4

Written by Viv Lambert ELT Limited
Additional material written by Tracy Traynor

This edition published 2021
First edition entitled *Story Central* published 2015 by Macmillan Education Limited.

Designed by Liz Adcock
Illustrated by Valentina Belloni (MB Artists) pp. 72–73; Robin Boyden (Pickled Ink) p. 56; Inna Chernyak (Plum Pudding) p. 24; Marcus Cutler (Sylvie Poggio Artist Agency) p. 64; Sarah Horne (Advocate Art) pp. 10, 15, 22, 25, 26, 28, 31, 34, 42, 44, 47, 50, 52, 54, 55, 58, 59, 66, 73, 74; Ellie Jenkins (Advocate Art) pp. 48–49; Andy Keylock (Beehive Illustration) pp. 6, 7, 10, 12–14, 18, 20, 26, 30, 34, 37, 39, 42, 50, 51, 55, 62, 70, 74, 75, 77, 78, 81, 82, 83, 85, 88, 90, 92, 95, 98, 101; Ayesha Lopez (Advocate Art) pp. 32–33; Louise Redshaw (Plum Pudding) pp16–17; Stephen Reed (The July Group) pp. 12, 14, 23, 27, 29, 39, 35, 38, 40, 41, 43, 46, 49, 58, 63, 65, 67, 69, 71, 76, 70, 79, 83, 84, 86, 87, 89, 91–94, 96; Steven Wood (Advocate Art) pp. 3–77; Patricia Yuste (Advocate Art) pp. 8–9.
Cover design by Wild Apple Design Ltd. and Roberto Martinez
Cover illustration Steven Wood (Advocate Art)
Picture research by Composure

Author's acknowledgements
Thank you to the team at Macmillan for their support and also to Tracy Traynor for her invaluable input and advice.

The authors and publishers would like to thank the following for permission to reproduce their photographs:
Alamy Stock Photo/Christopher Bradshaw (tr)p. 83; **Macmillan Education Limited** p. 80; Macmillan Education Limited/Paul Bricknell (tc)p. 83; Macmillan Education Limited/Alamy Stock Photo/NordicImages (tl)p.83.

Printed and bound in Brazil.

2025

41

Contents

Welcome to Story Central

1 **Draw you with Libby. Then complete for you.**

Hi, I'm Libby. What's your name?

My name's ....

How old are you?

I'm ....

2 **Match.**

a b c d

Ellie Libby Biblio Tom

3 Read and color.

8 6 3 9

Color *three* black.

Color *nine* pink.

Color *six* purple.

Color *eight* red.

4 Circle the letters in the wrong place. Write the circled letters to make a color.

1 a b c d b

2 e f g l i

3 l m n a p

4 q r c t u

5 k w x y z

b _ _ _ _

5 Write and draw two more English words you know.

Chapter 1 My School

Lesson 1

1 **Complete the puzzle. Find who is behind the door.**

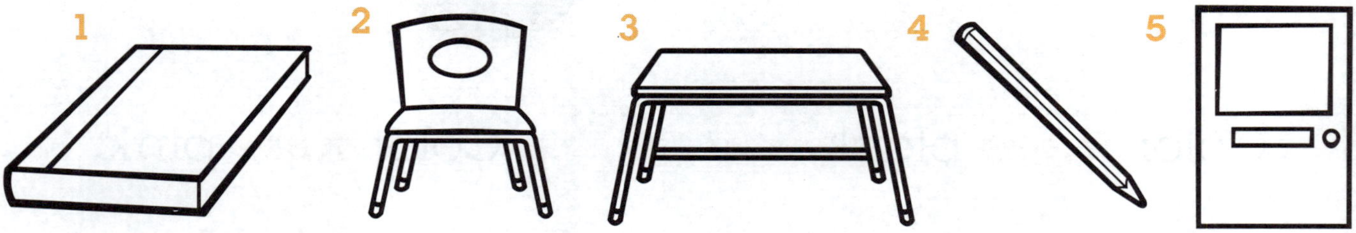

2 **Write the words in two groups.**

~~door~~
table
chair
pencil
book
pen

big things	small things
door	

Lesson 2

1 Draw and write. Then ask and answer.

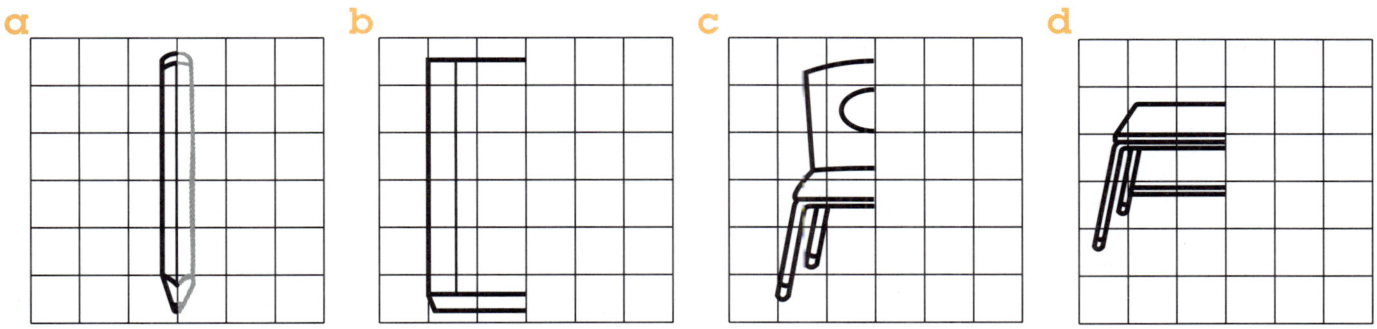

1 [ ] It's a table.
2 [ ] It's a chair.
3 [a] It's a pencil.
4 [ ] It's a book.

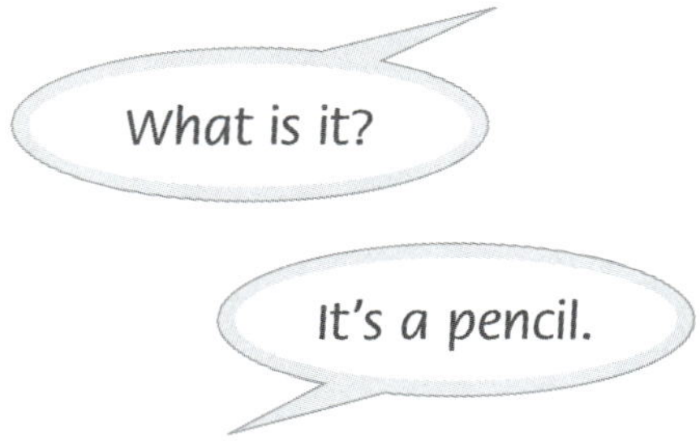

2 Look and complete.

1  Is it a chair? Yes, it is.

2 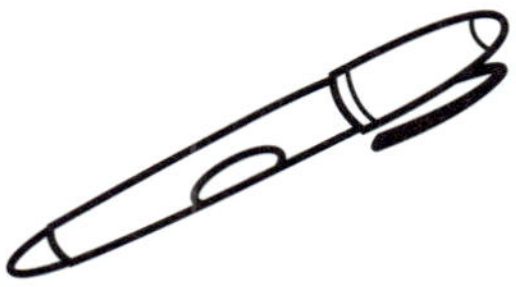 .... it a pencil? ...., it isn't.

3 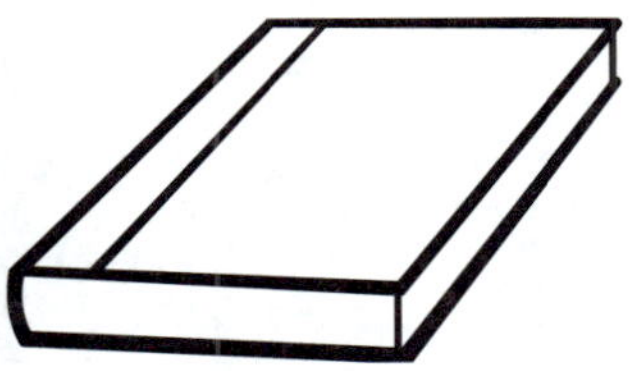 .... it a book? Yes, ...

4  .... a door? ....

Lesson 3

1 Number in order. Then act out.

☐ I'm fine, thank you.
How are you, [name]?

☐ Hello, [name].
How are you?

☐ I'm fine too, thanks.

2 Read the story in your Student Book. Circle T (true) or F (false).

1 The boy's name is Chen. **T / F**

2 Chen draws a table. **T / F**

3 The girl has a book. **T / F**

4 The pen isn't magic. **T / F**

3 What happens next? Choose and check (✔).

☐

☐

☐

Lesson 4
Time to Think

1 **Look and complete. Then number in story order.**

rice
tree
~~horse~~
door

☐ It's a horse.

☐ It's a ______.

☐ It's ______.

1 It's a ______.

2 **Draw a front cover for the storybook.**

I Can Read!

Chen's Magic Pen

Ruth Stitt

3 **Do you like the story? Choose and circle.**

Yes! ☺ No. ☹ I'm not sure. 😐

Lesson 5

1 **Circle six words for school items.**

p e n c i l c a s e r u l e r n o t e b o o k e r a s e r b a g c r a y o n

2 **Write the items from Activity 1 with *a* or *an* in the correct place.**

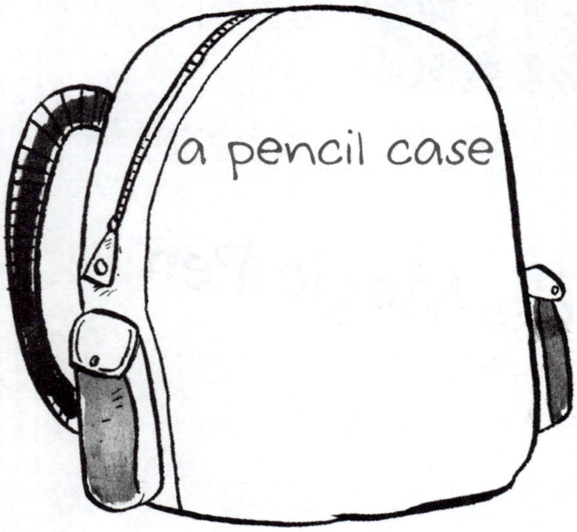

3 **Say the words. Circle *p* as in *pen*.**

p

pen book pencil pink

blue purple pencil case

Lesson 6

1 Write a list of items for school.

a notebook

2 Match.

1 What color
2 It's
3 An orange
4 It

a notebook.
b isn't an eraser.
c is the pencil?
d blue.

3 Draw items from Activity 1. Then complete and color.

1 What color is the notebook? It's red.

2 ______ color is the ______? ______ yellow.

3 It isn't a pencil. It's a blue ______.

4 It ______ ruler. It's an ______.

Lesson 7 CLIL

1 Why are trees important? Match.

2 Use your Student Book research. Complete the Tree Poster.

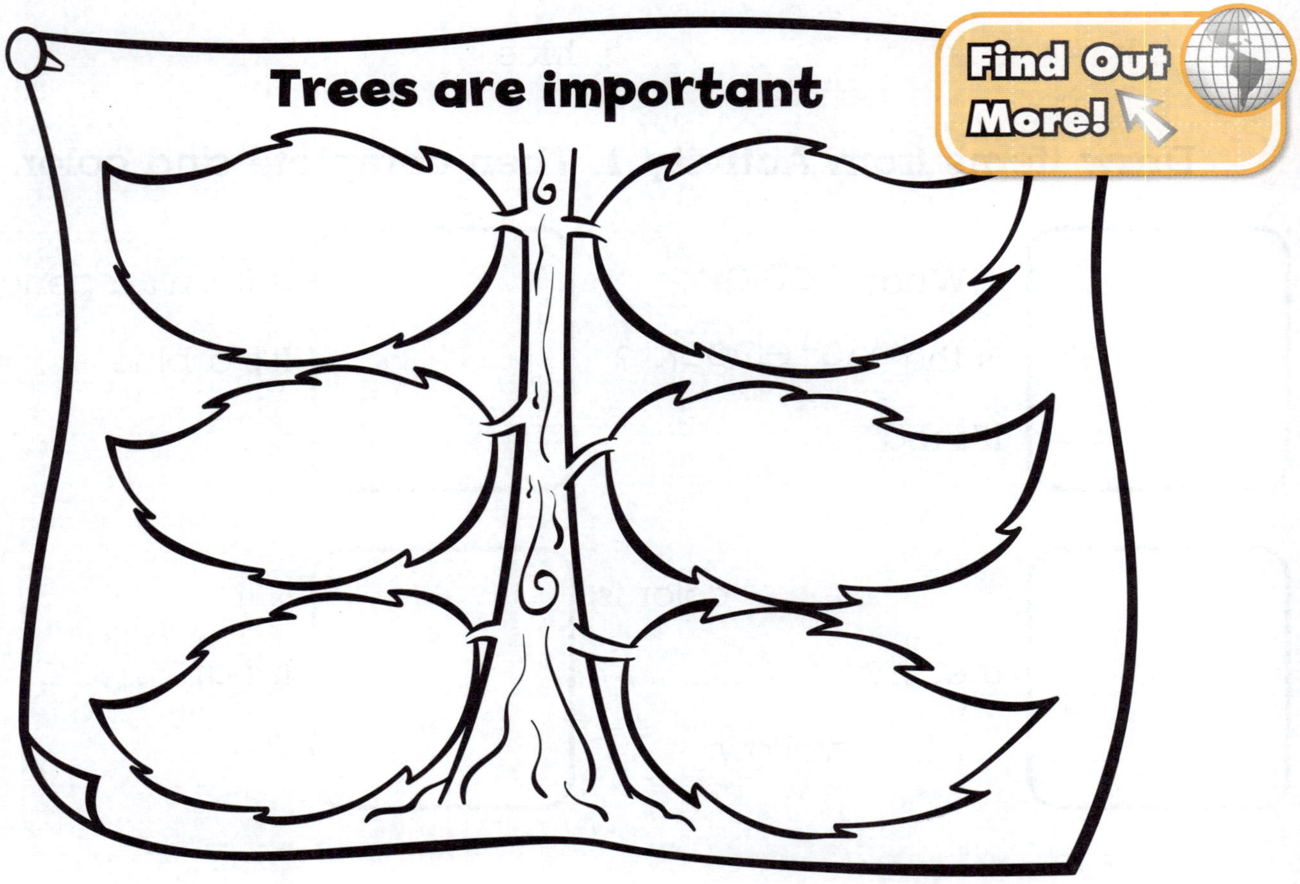

1 Read and color.

1 = orange
3 = green
5 = purple
2 = blue
4 = yellow
6 = red

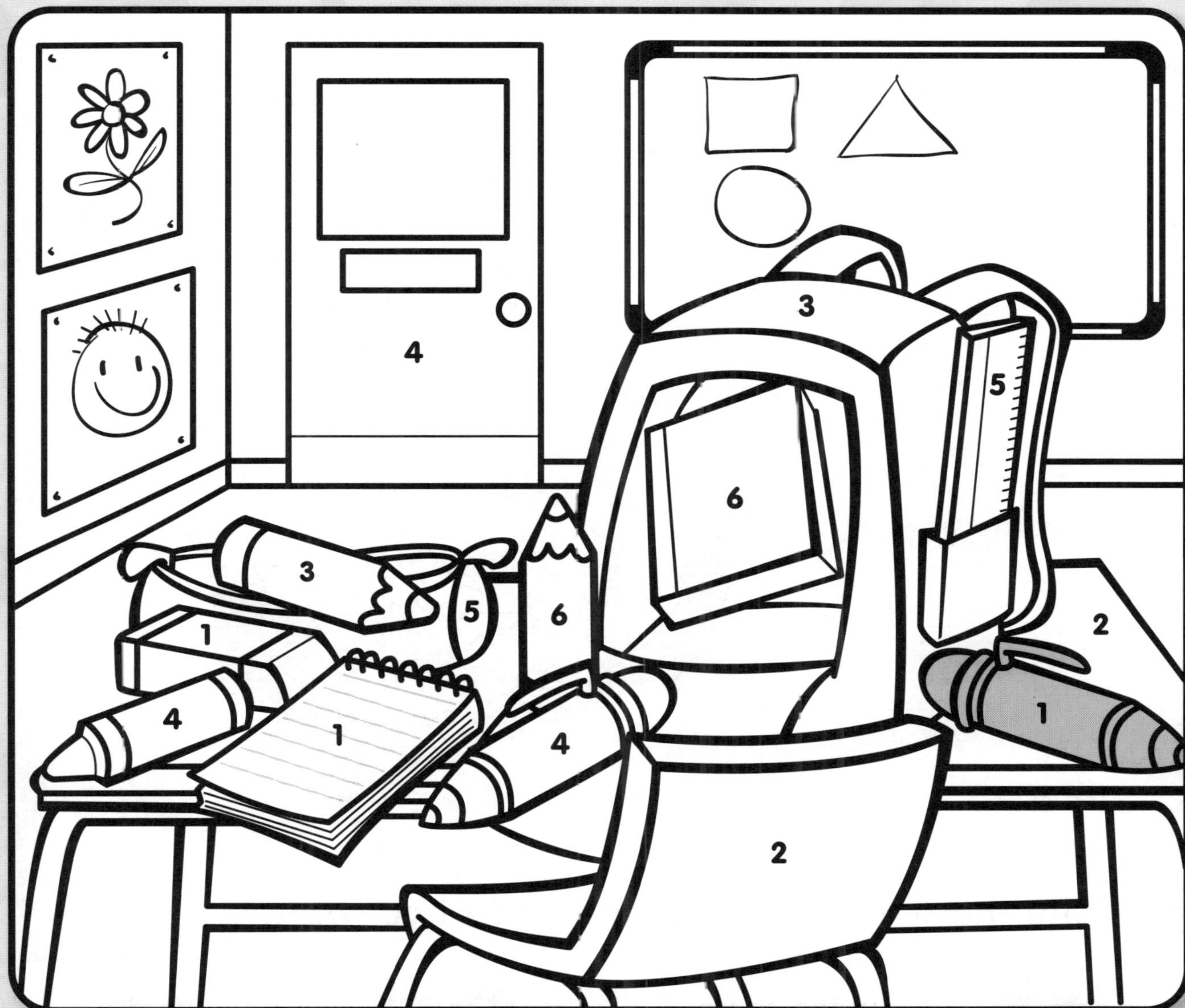

2 Play a game. Ask and answer.

Chapter 2 My Toys

Lesson 1

1 Circle and match. Then use the extra letters to find and write Biblio's favorite toy.

r c a r o d o l l b b a l l o t e d d y b e a r t b i k e

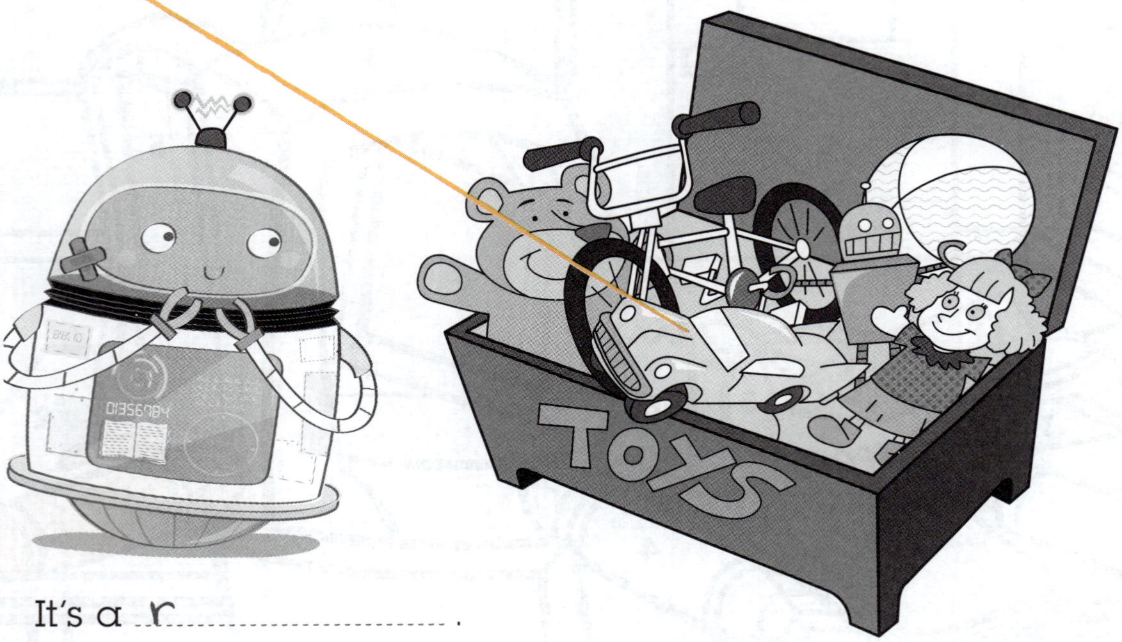

It's a r..

2 Write the words from Activity 1 in two groups.

in the house	in the yard
a doll	

1 Complete with *This is* or *That's*.

1 This is my car.
2 That's my doll.
3 .... my bike.
4 .... my teddy bear.
5 .... my ball.
6 .... my robot.

2 Write the questions and answers.

Yes, it is. No, it isn't.

1 robot? / your / Is / this — Is this your robot?
(✔) — Yes, it is.

2 your / Is / bike? / that — .... ?
(✔) — ....

3 this / doll? / your / Is — .... ?
(✘) — ....

4 car? / Is / your / that — .... ?
(✘) — ....

Lesson 3

favorite
this
small

1 Complete. Then act out.

Hello! Is .... your book?

Yes, it is.

What's your .... toy?

My car. It's .... and red.

2 Read the story in your Student Book. Circle Polly's answers.

1 What's your favorite toy? My **doll** / **teddy bear**.

2 How old are you? I'm **4** / **13**.

3 Is this your teddy bear? No. My teddy bear is **brown** / **yellow**.

4 Is this your teddy bear? No. My teddy bear is **small** / **big**.

3 What happens next? Choose and check (✓).

☐

☐

☐

Lesson 4
Time to Think

1 **Read and color. Then complete with *big* or *small*.**

1 It's .... and green.

2 It's .... and brown.

3 It's .... and yellow.

2 **Write the title.**

princess the teddy bear and the

I Can Read!

3 **Do you like the story? Choose and circle.**

Yes! No. I'm not sure.

Lesson 5

1 **Write the missing months in order.**

May | October | ~~February~~ | December | July

January	February	March	April
....	June	....	August
September	....	November	....

2 **When's Ellie's birthday? Read and write.**

It isn't in January, June, or July.

It isn't in August.

It isn't in March or May.

It isn't in November or December.

It isn't in February, April, or October.

Ellie's birthday is in ....

3 **Say the words. Circle *j* as in *January*.**

j

January | July

chair | June | King Jade

orange | green

1 Write about you.

What's your name? My name's ....

How old are you? ....

When's your birthday? ....

What's your favorite toy? ....

2 Ask a friend the questions in Activity 1. Then write his/her answers.

What's his/her name? ....

How old is he/she? ....

When's his/her birthday? ....

What's his/her favorite toy? ....

3 Draw and write a birthday card for your friend.

Dear .... ,

It's ....

You're .... today.

Happy .... !

Lesson 7
CLIL

1 Read and color. Then count and write.

The circles are red.

The triangles are green.

The rectangles are yellow.

The squares are blue.

6 circles ______ triangles ______ rectangles ______ squares

2 Use your Student Book research. Make a Shape Page.

Find Out More!

Shape ______	Shape ______
Shape ______	Shape ______

Lesson 8

1 Choose and circle to make questions.

1 How old is your **brother** / **sister** / **dog**?

2 Draw a **square** / **triangle** / **rectangle**.

3 What's your favorite **toy** / **book** / **color**?

4 Name the months beginning with **J** / **M** / **A**.

5 Is this your **pen** / **book** / **pencil case**?

6 What's **4 + 9** / **9 + 8** / **10 + 5**?

2 Play the game. Roll the dice. Ask, answer, and color.

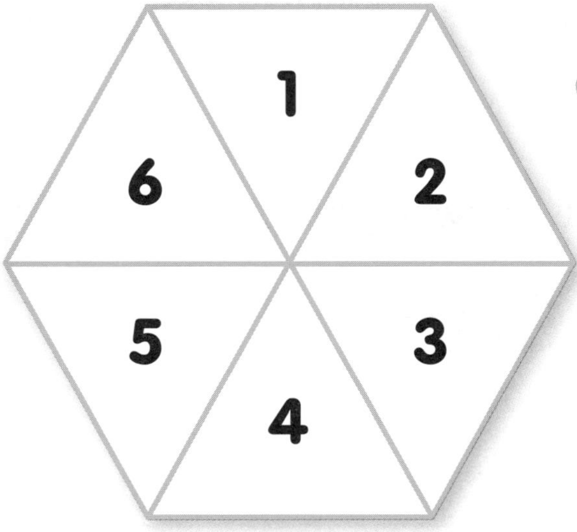

Six.

What's four and nine?

Thirteen!

Great! Color number six.

Chapter 3 Wild Animals

Lesson 1

1 Find and circle. Write.

m	c	j	c	u	r	e	o	a
e	g	i	r	a	f	f	e	l
l	e	d	o	p	y	i	o	b
e	p	h	c	p	d	s	r	w
p	z	m	o	n	k	e	y	l
h	q	b	d	q	e	l	t	g
a	h	r	i	s	a	i	v	i
n	x	t	l	s	u	o	a	f
t	i	g	e	r	k	n	v	n

1 monkey

2 ....

3 ....

4 ....

5 ....

6 ....

2 Write the words from Activity 1 in two groups.

easy words	difficult words

1 Count and write.

1 three giraffes

2 ....

3 ....

4 ....

5 ....

2 Look and write. Then ask and answer.

1 What are these?

They're giraffes.

3 What are .... ?

....

2 What are those ?

They're ....

4 .... ?

....

Lesson 3

1 Choose and circle. Then act out.

Let's look at **these** / **those** books about **cars** / **toys**.

No. Let's look at **these** / **those** books about **animals** / **colors**.

OK.

2 Read the story in your Student Book. Circle T (true) or F (false).

1 The giraffe is happy. **T / F**

2 The baby giraffe is very tall. **T / F**

3 The elephant is hungry. **T / F**

4 The trees are very tall. **T / F**

3 What happens next? Choose and check (✔).

Lesson 4
Time to Think

1 Find and circle seven words. Then use the words to complete the sentences.

g i r a f f e n e c k t a l l t r e e s g r e e n l e a v e s h u n g r y

1 I'm hungry .

2 These .... are brown. Those leaves are ....

3 The .... are very ....

4 My .... !

5 Thank you, ...

2 Number in order to make a sentence. Write.

green are the but Those tall leaves are trees

green	are	the	but	Those	tall	leaves	are	trees
				1				

Those ....

3 Do you like the story? Choose and circle.

Yes! No. I'm not sure.

Lesson 5

1 Write the words in the circles.

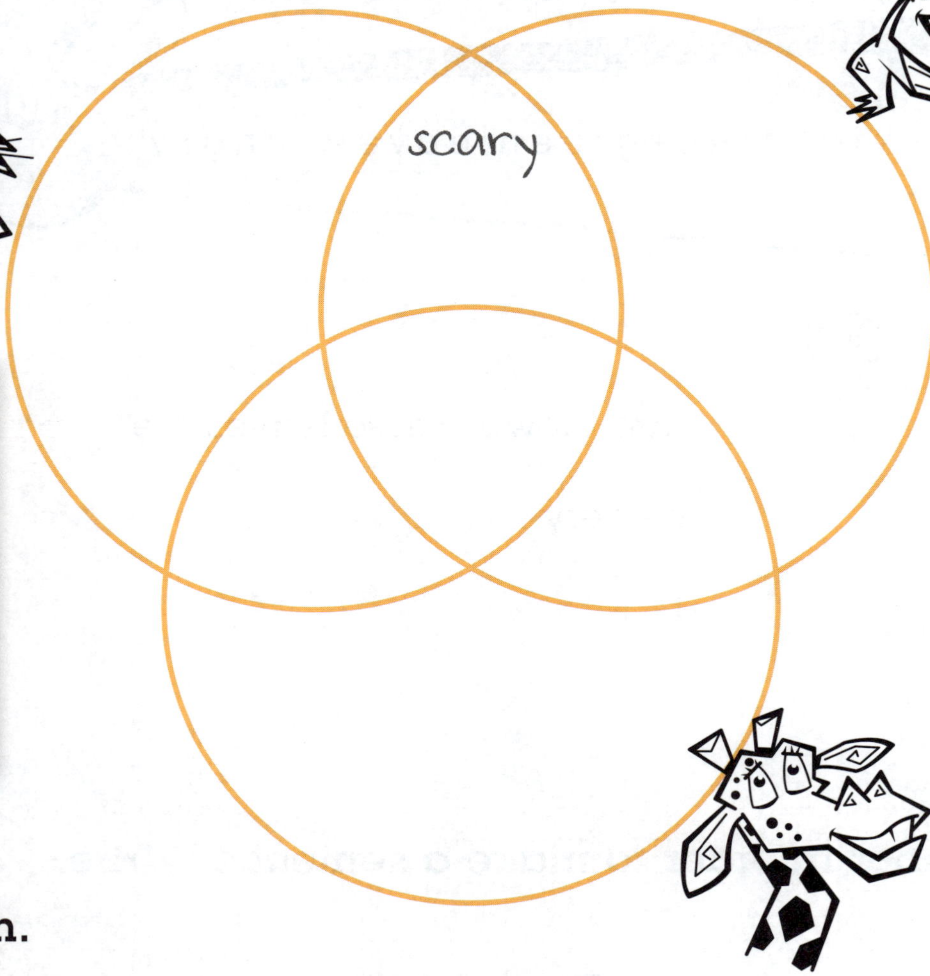

~~scary~~	green
tall	white
long	orange
thin	brown
hungry	black
big	animal

2 Match.

1 Giraffes	a are long and green.
2 Monkeys	b are tall and thin.
3 Crocodiles	c are big and gray.
4 Elephants	d are small and brown.

3 Say the words. Circle *t* as in *tall*.

trees tall hungry
snappy long tiger

1 Look and circle.

1 It's / They're elephants.
2 They're black / gray.
3 They're big / small.
4 They are / aren't scary.

2 Choose an animal. Draw and complete the Fact File.

FACT FILE

Animal: ....

Color: ....

big / small

scary / cute

They are ....

They aren't ....

3 Answer for your animal.

1 Are they gray? ....
2 Are they small? ....
3 Are they scary? ....
4 Are they cute? ....

Lesson 7 CLIL

1 **Complete the text.**

- animals
- hungry
- ~~crocodile~~
- those
- giraffes

What's this? It's a crocodile. Crocodiles eat meat.

Can you see .... giraffes? Watch out, ... !

This crocodile is ....

Crocodiles eat giraffes and other ....

2 **Use your Student Book research. Make a food chart for another animal.**

Find Out More!

My animal	This animal eats	This animal is

1 **Choose an animal. Ask and answer to complete the path.**

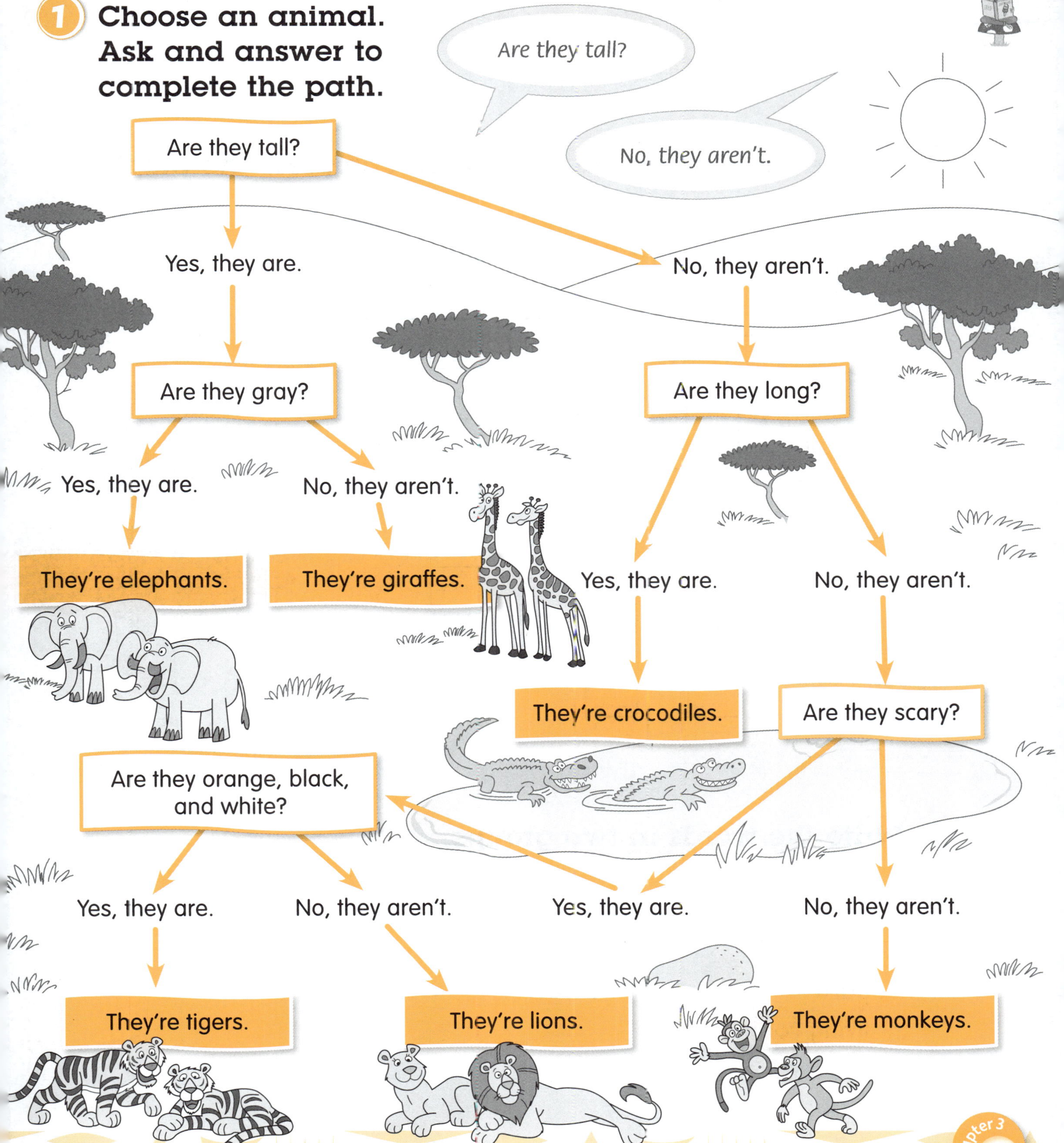

Chapter 4 My House

Lesson 1

1 **Where do you find these things? Complete the puzzle.**

1

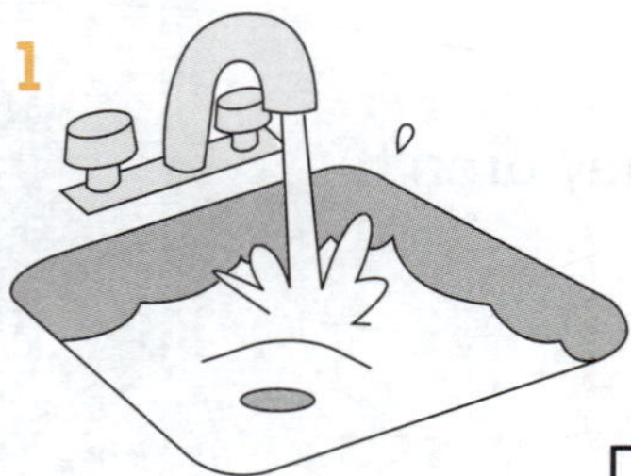

2

3

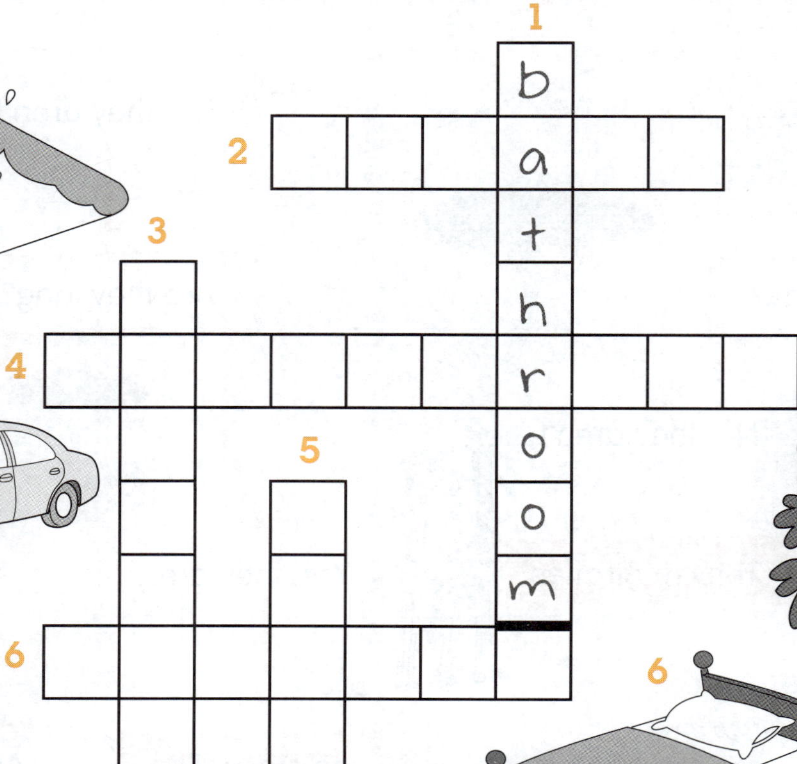

4

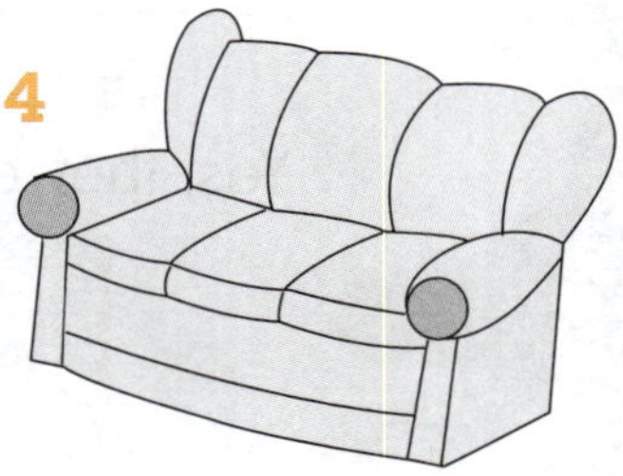

5

6

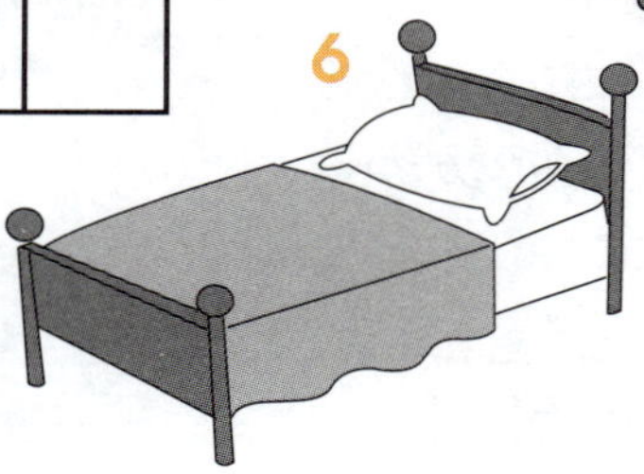

2 **Write the words in two groups.**

~~bedroom~~
bathroom
yard
living room
kitchen
garage

inside the house	outside the house
bedroom	

1 Look and complete.

in
on
~~under~~
behind

1 The teddy bear is ....under.......... the chair.

2 The car is .... the table.

3 The monkey is .... the bag.

4 The ruler is .... the monkey.

2 Now complete and match.

1 ....Where's.......... the doll?

2 Where's the bag?

3 Where's the ball?

4 .... ruler?

a It's in the bag.

b It's .... the table.

c It's under the table.

d It's .... the bag.

3 Draw a cat and a mouse in the picture. Then ask and answer.

Where's the cat?

Lesson 3

1 Choose and circle. Then act out.

Can I listen to the story, too?

No, sorry. / Sit here. / Yes, of course.

2 Read the story in your Student Book. Complete the sentences about the cat.

's
~~behind~~
table
isn't

1 The cat is behind the door in the living room.

2 It isn't under the ______________ .

3 It ______________ in the kitchen.

4 It ______________ in the bedroom.

3 Why is Max in the scary house? Choose and check (✓).

☐

☐

☐

1 Draw the necklace. Then draw the cat's route through the house.

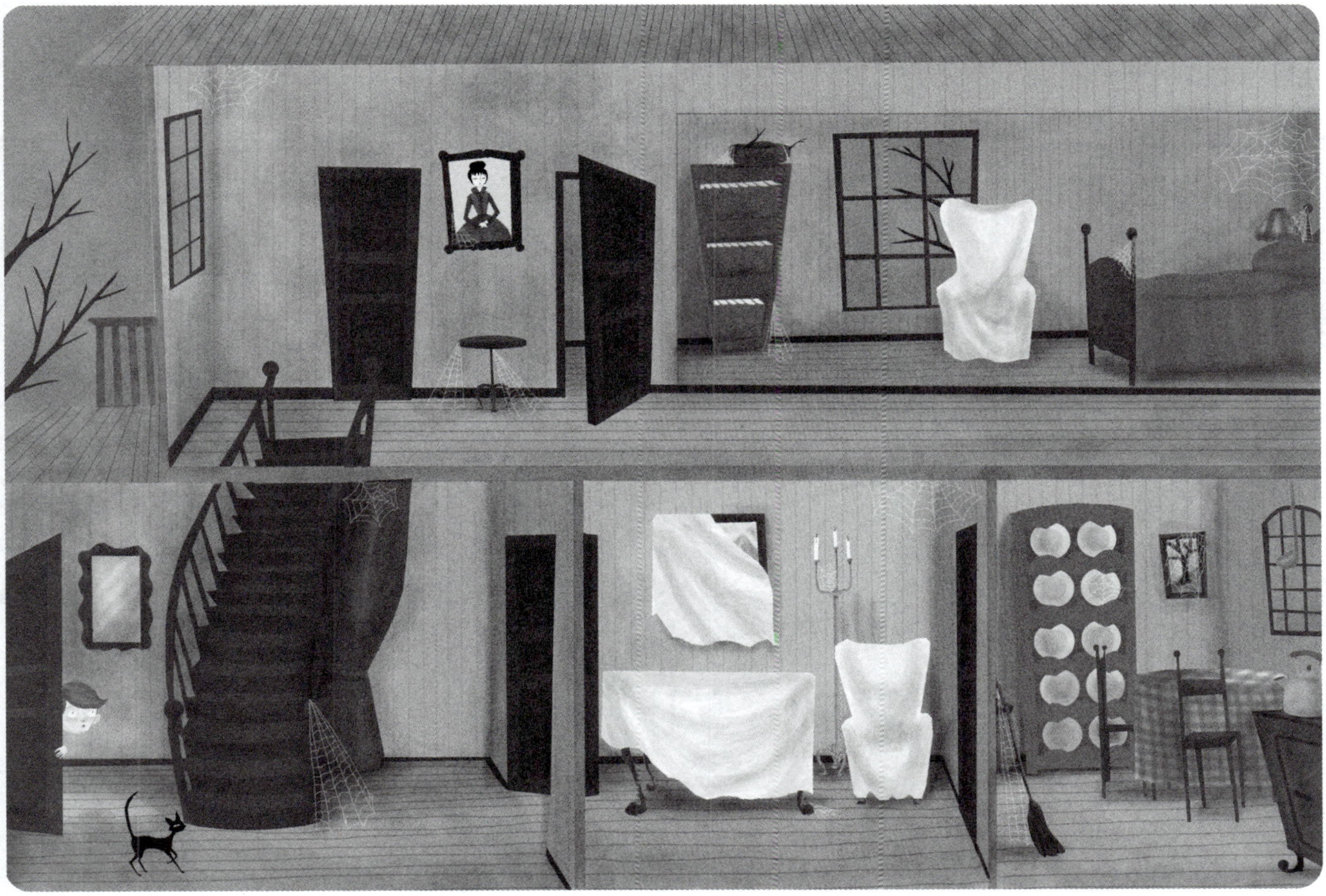

2 Complete with "?" or "."

I Can Read!

1 Can I come in ...?...
2 What's that ....
3 It's a cat ....
4 It's in the bedroom ....
5 What's on the shelf ....
6 Is this your cat ....

3 Do you like the story? Choose and circle.

Yes! No. I'm not sure.

Lesson 5

bed shelf desk TV ~~closet~~ sofa floor

1 Write.

1 closet 2 ________ 3 ________

4 ________

5 ________ 6 ________ 7 ________

2 Read and draw these things in the picture.

1 A car is under the bed.

2 A cat is in the closet.

3 A ball is behind the TV.

4 A teddy bear is on the sofa.

3 Say the words. Circle *l* as in *living*. Underline *r* as in *room*.

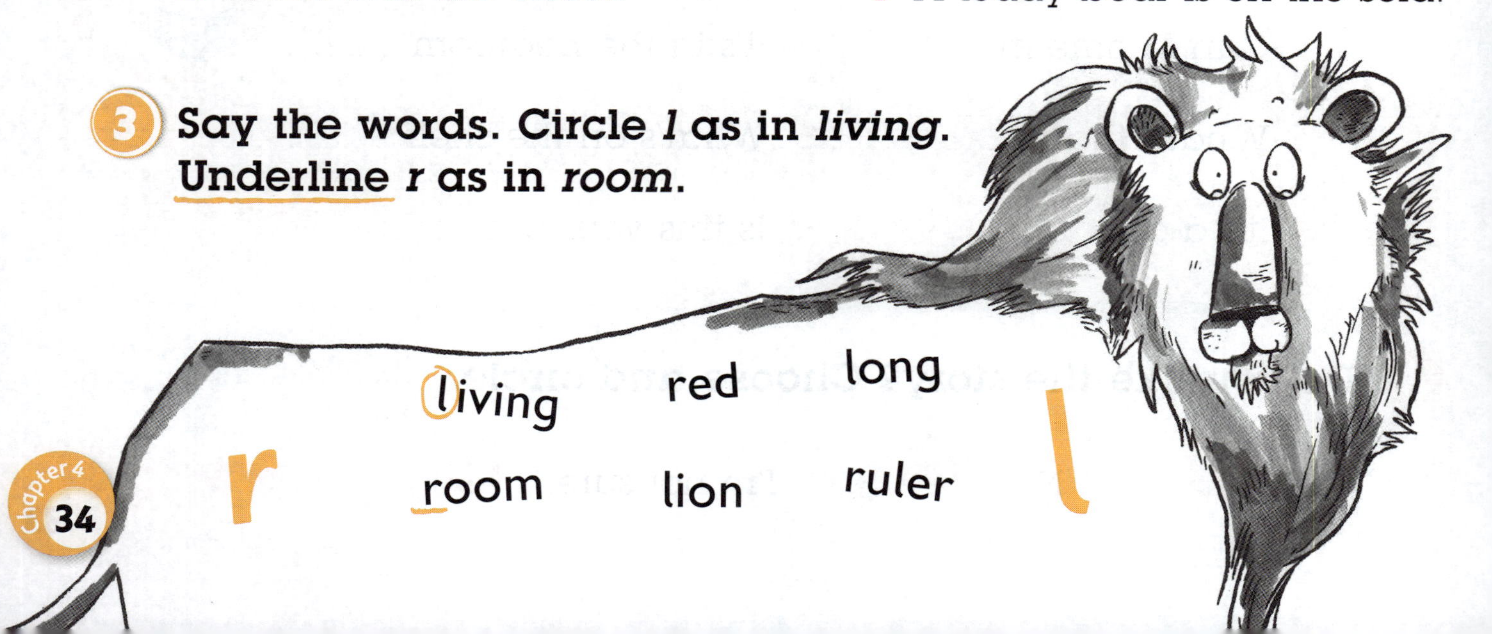

r

living red long

room lion ruler

l

1 Read and write the opposite instructions.

1 Stand up. Don't stand up.

2 Don't sit down. ....

3 Open the book. ....

4 Don't look. ....

2 Circle the instructions to find the clue.

Sit down / **Don't sit down** on the floor.

What can you see?

Look **on** / **under** the **chair** / **bed**.

It begins with **b** / **c** / **e**.

3 Hide an eraser in the classroom. Circle and complete the instructions for a friend to find it.

Stand .... the chair.

What .... see?

Look in / on / under / behind the ....

It begins with ....

Lesson 7 CLIL

1 **What's in your home? Check (✔).**

- living room ☐
- bedrooms ☐
- yard ☐
- kitchen ☐
- bathroom ☐
- garage ☐

2 **Ask 10 friends and complete. Then count.**

I live in . . .			
	a house	an apartment	other
Total			

Do you live in a house?

No, I don't. I live in an apartment.

3 **Use your Student Book research. Draw an unusual home and label the rooms.**

Find Out More!

1 How many cats can you find? Circle and count.

2 Draw cats in different colors for a friend to find.

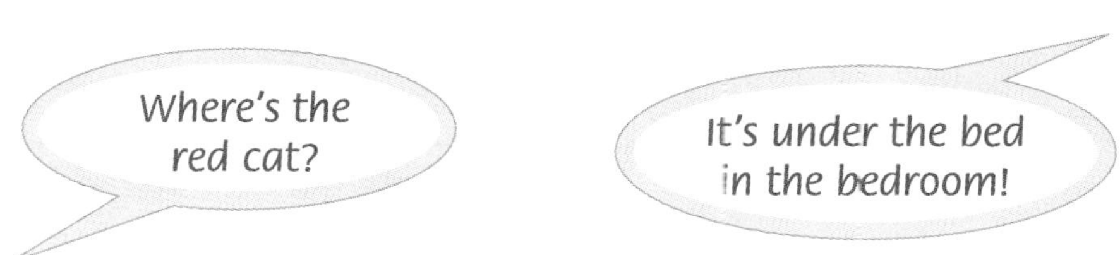

Chapter 5 My Town

Lesson 1

1 Number. Then draw the missing place in the picture.

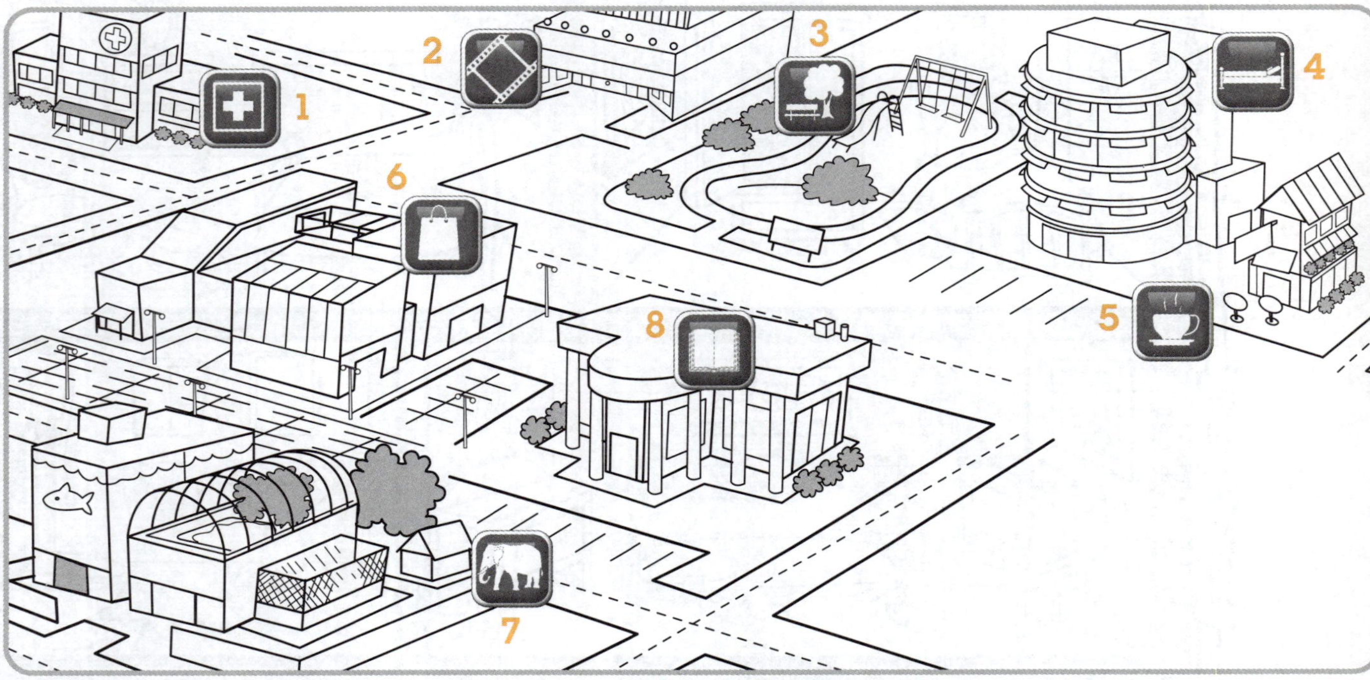

movie theater	2	café		hotel	
zoo		hospital		library	
swimming pool		mall		park	

2 Write the words from Activity 1 in two groups.

I like this place.	I don't like this place.

1 Look and complete with *There's* or *There isn't*.

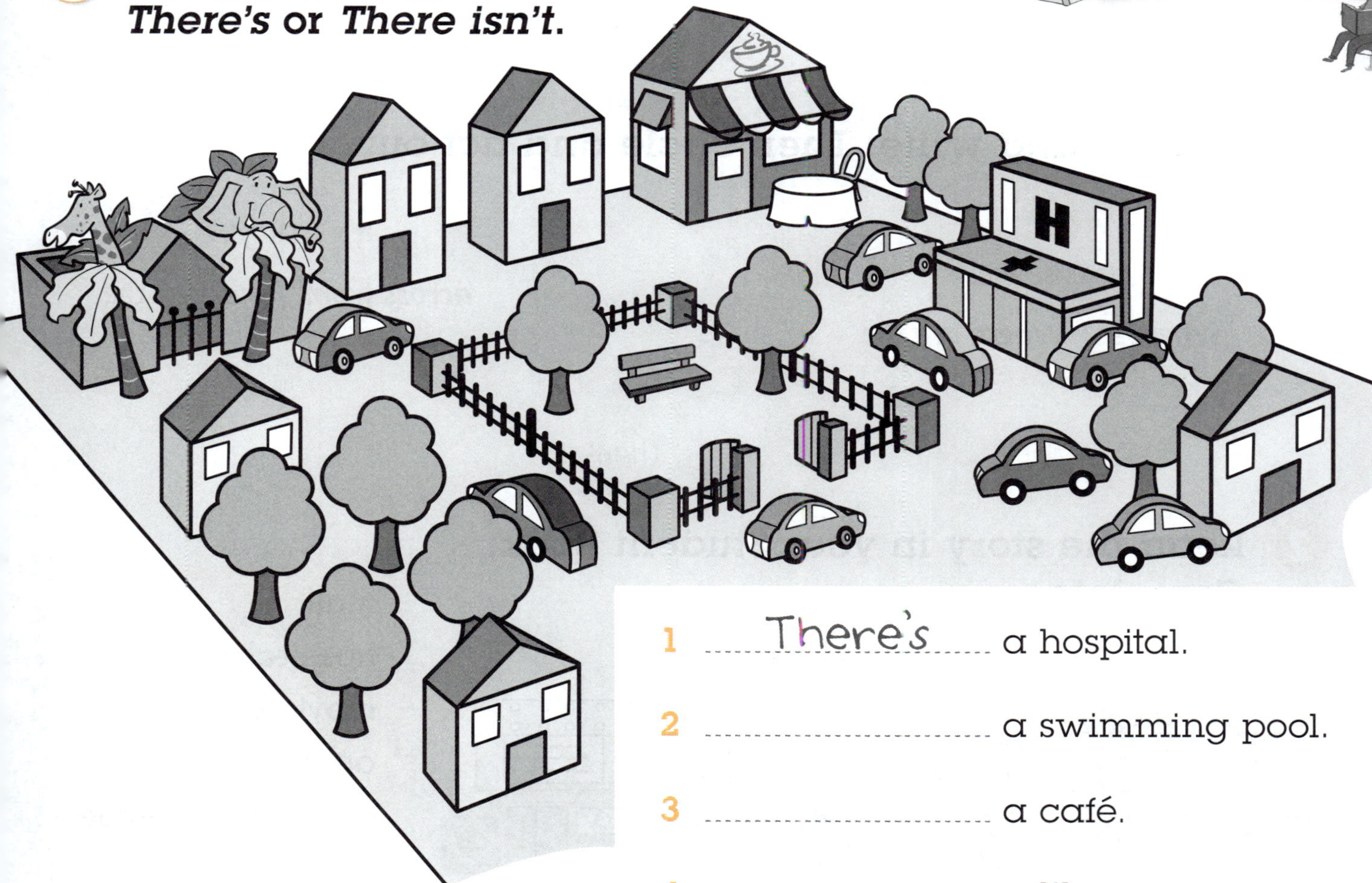

1 There's a hospital.

2 .... a swimming pool.

3 .... a café.

4 .... a library.

2 Look at the picture in Activity 1. Complete the questions and circle the answers.

1 Is there a zoo? **Yes, there is.** / **No, there isn't.**

2 .... movie theater? **Yes, there is.** / **No, there isn't.**

3 .... hotel? **Yes, there is.** / **No, there isn't.**

3 Look again. Count and write.

1 How many cars are there? There are ....

2 .... trees .... ? ....

Lesson 3

1 Choose and write. Then circle and act out.

Excuse me!
Where's / **Where are** the ______________ ?

It's / **They're**
across from / **next to** the
______________ .

Thanks!

2 Read the story in your Student Book. Complete.

mall
~~hospital~~
movie theater
on First Avenue
on Second Avenue

1 2 3

1 Where's the hospital ? It's on First Avenue.

2 Where's the ______________ ? ______________ .

3 Where's the ______________ ? ______________ .

3 What's this man going to do? Choose and check (✔).

1 Match. Then number the places in the story order.

bus station ☐ mall 1 police station ☐ park ☐

I Can Read!

2 Which words are like *Whoosh!*? Draw ☆ around those words.

ZOOM! HELLO! CRASH! Excuse me! CLICK!

3 Do you like the story? Choose and circle.

Yes! No. I'm not sure.

Lesson 5

1 Circle the one that doesn't belong.

1	bus	street	van
2	truck	three	five
3	van	motorcycle	mall
4	library	taxi	car

2 Write the words in the correct outlines.

bus
van
~~motorcycle~~
truck
taxi
car

3 Say the words. Circle *b* as in *bus*. Underline *v* as in *vroom*.

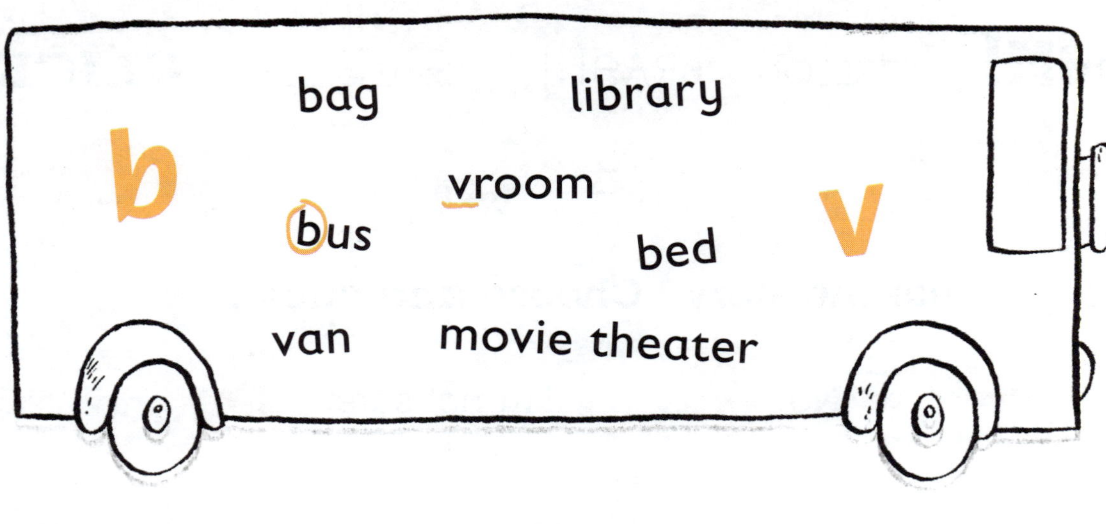

Lesson 6

1 Look at the map. You're in the taxi. Read, follow the directions, and write.

1 Go straight.
Take the second right.
It's across from the park.
Where are you?
I'm at the ______.

2 Take the first left.
Take the first right.
It's next to the movie theater.
Where are you?
______.

2 Look at the map in Activity 1. Complete for the library and the café.

1 Take the first left ______.
Go ______.
The library is ______
the bus station.

2 Take the ______ right.
Take the first ______.
The café is ______
the hospital.

Lesson 7 CLIL

1 What transportation is there in Bangkok? Write.

river buses ~~cars and taxis~~ motorcycles tuk-tuks

1 There are a lot of these. cars and taxis

2 They're blue and red. ______________

3 They have two wheels. ______________

4 They're on the river. ______________

2 Use your Student Book research. Make a Transportation Poster.

Find Out More!

1 Look and say the directions with a friend.

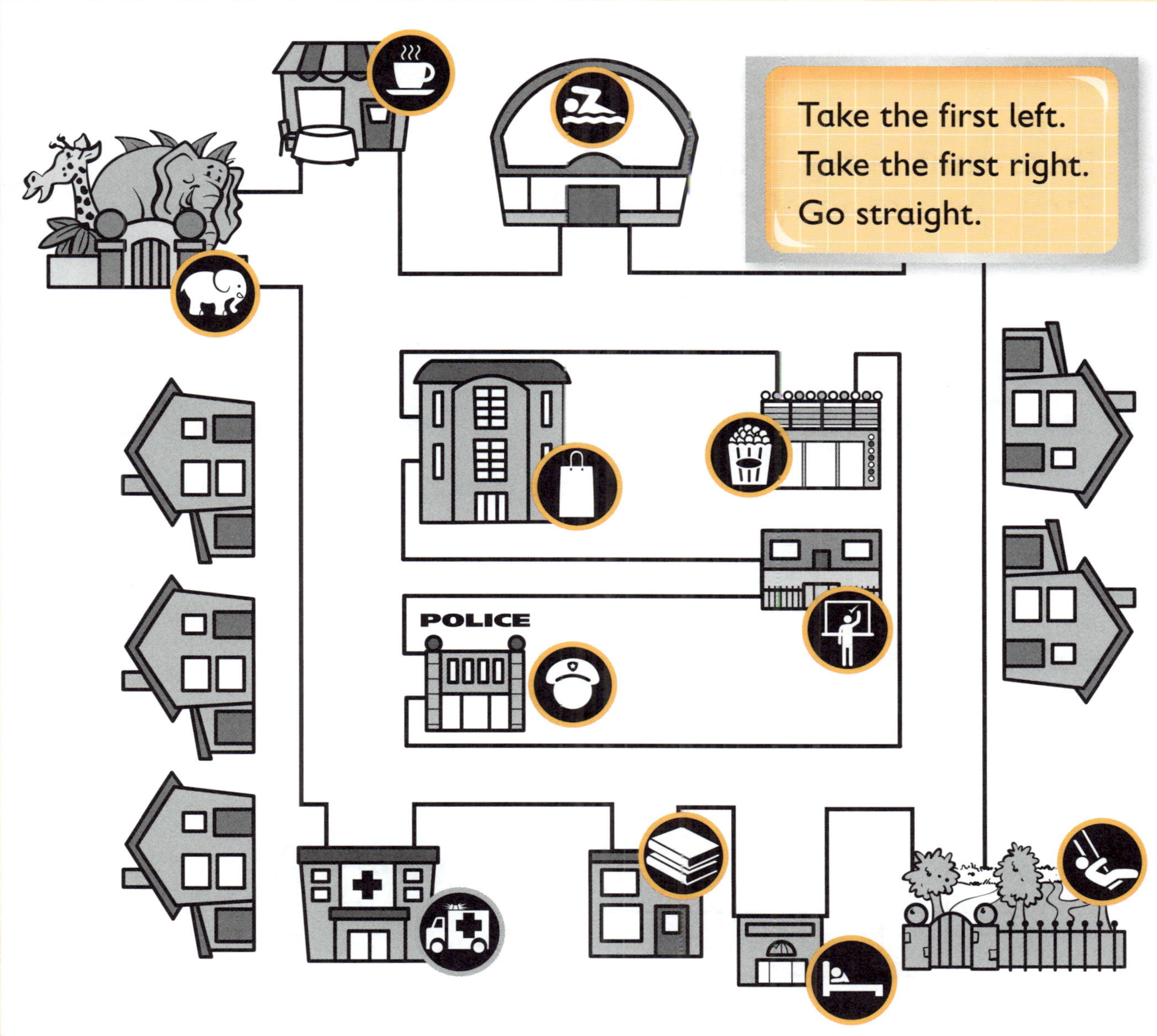

zoo ☞ library **park** ☞ **swimming pool**

hospital ☞ ***movie theater*** hotel ☞ café

Zoo to library. Take the first right at the café.

Go straight at the mall.

Chapter 6 My Family

Lesson 1

1 **Unscramble the words and complete the puzzle. Find the name of Jack's dad.**

1 elcnu 2 rteiss 3 rboreth 4 aamrgnd 5 tuna 6 pragdan 7 add 8 mmo Jack

My dad's name is ....

2 **Write the words from Activity 1 in two groups.**

male	female
uncle	

~~uncle~~
mom
dad
sister
grandma
brother
grandpa
aunt

1 Look and complete with *I have* or *I don't have*.

1 I have .... a mom and a dad.

2 I don't have .... any sisters.

3 .... two brothers.

4 .... two grandmas.

5 .... a grandpa.

6 .... any aunts or uncles.

2 Draw a picture of your family. Then write.

I have ....

....

Lesson 3

1 Number in order. Then act out.

- Hello, Maria. [ ]
- Hi, Maria. This is my little sister, Sophie. [ ]
- Hello, Jack. Who's this? [1]
- Hi, Sophie. Nice to meet you! [ ]

2 Read the story in your Student Book. Circle.

1 I have a **big** / **small** family.

2 I **have** / **don't have** a sister.

3 The turnip is **big** / **small**.

4 Olga is **happy** / **hungry**.

3 What happens next? Choose and check (✔).

[ ]

[ ]

[ ]

1 Complete the family tree.

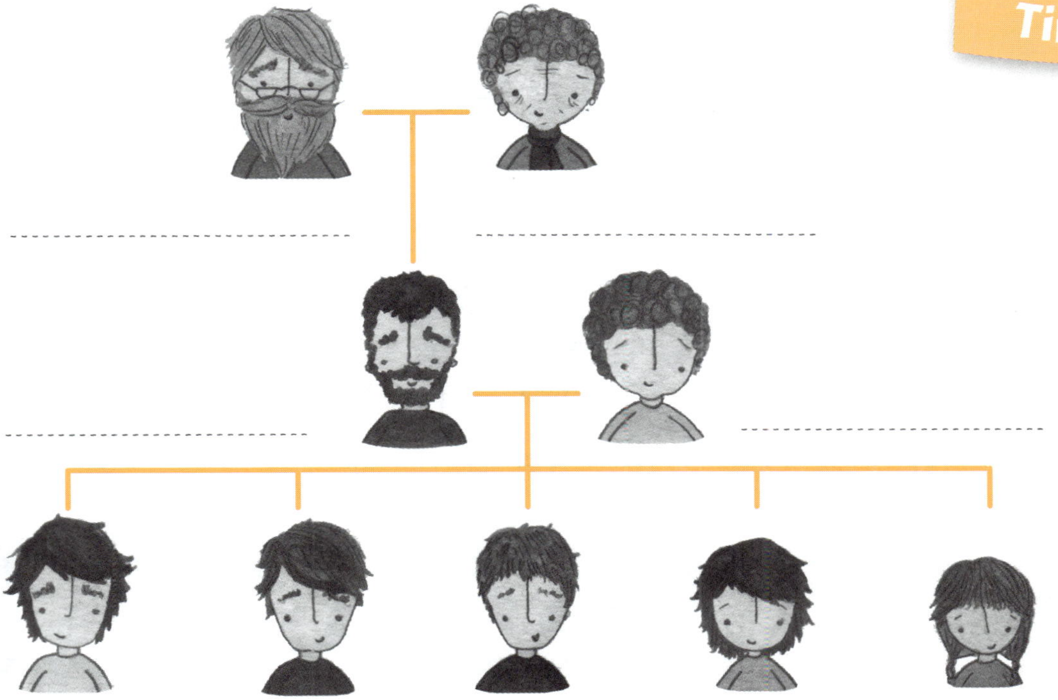

Mikhail

~~Mikhail~~
Yuri
grandma
Sergei
dad
Olga
grandpa
Nadia
mom

2 Write the words in the speech bubbles.

I Can Read!

HOORAY! HELP! STOP!

3 Do you like the story? Choose and circle.

Yes! No. I'm not sure.

Lesson 5

1 **Find and circle.**

g	c	f	q	f	r	o	g
h	a	m	s	t	e	r	w
m	t	o	i	h	b	h	l
o	b	d	o	g	s	f	e
u	i	r	a	b	b	i	t
s	r	t	r	j	a	s	b
e	d	s	a	m	e	h	p
t	u	r	t	l	e	x	t

2 **Write the words from Activity 1 in alphabetical order. Then number.**

bird 6

3 **Say the words. Circle *h* as in *hamster*.**

hamster

have

June

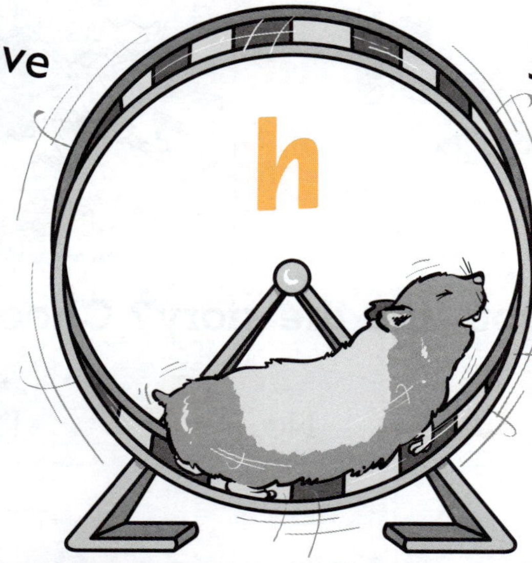

aunt

house

hungry

giraffe

1 Circle.

1 What's your / my name? **Their** / **My** name's Jake.

2 Do you have **no** / **any** brothers or sisters? Yes, **I do** / **I don't**.

I have a brother.

3 **Do you** / **You do** have any aunts or uncles? No, **I do** / **I don't**.

4 **Are you** / **Do you** have any pets? Yes, I do.

2 Complete the email.

house Their brother cat ~~Sam~~

Hi [your name] ....,

My name's Sam. I'm in Sydney.

I love Australia. I have a small ....

and a yard.

I have a .... His name is Bobby.

I don't have a sister. I have a .... and a dog.

.... names are Flo and Bonzo.

Write soon.

Love,

Sam

Lesson 7 CLIL

1 Complete the poster.

Do you have ....?

Do you love ....?

.... is hungry.

Please help. Give ....

a bed and ....

2 Use your Student Book research. Draw your animal and complete the Fact File.

Find Out More!

FACT FILE

My animal is a

....

It needs

....

....

Lesson 8

1 Play the game. Roll the dice and draw.

Key:

1 = a brother
2 = a sister
3 = a cat
4 = a dog
5 = a hamster
6 = a fish

2 Look at your house. Talk to a friend.

Do you have any pets?

Yes, I do. I have two cats.

Chapter 7 Strange Creatures

Lesson 1

1 **Circle. Then write.**

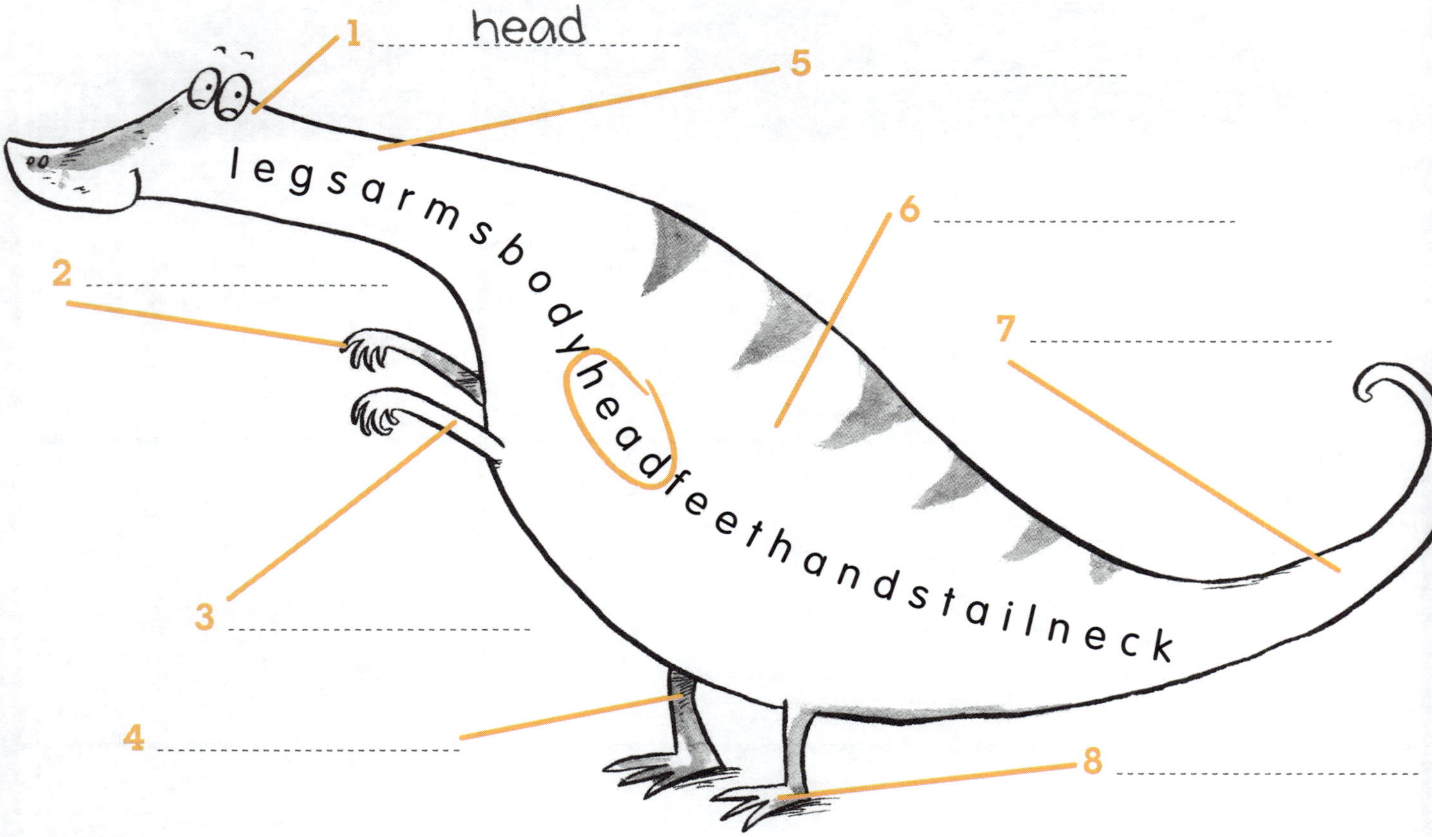

2 **Write the words from Activity 1 in three groups for you.**

I have one	I have two	I don't have a
head		

Lesson 2

1 Look, read, and check (✔) or cross (✗).

1 It has a big body. ✔

2 It has two legs. ☐

3 It doesn't have any arms. ☐

4 It has two hands. ☐

5 It doesn't have a tail. ☐

6 It has a long neck. ☐

2 Write about this animal.

It has ....

It has ....

It doesn't have ....

3 Choose an animal and write. Then play a guessing game.

It has ....

....

It doesn't have ....

....

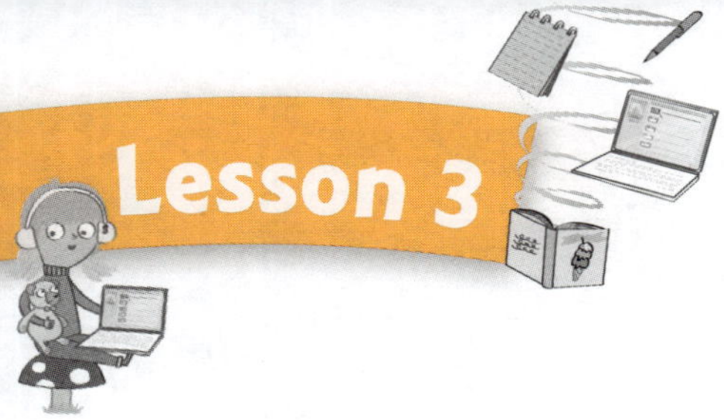

Lesson 3

1 **Choose and circle. Then act out.**

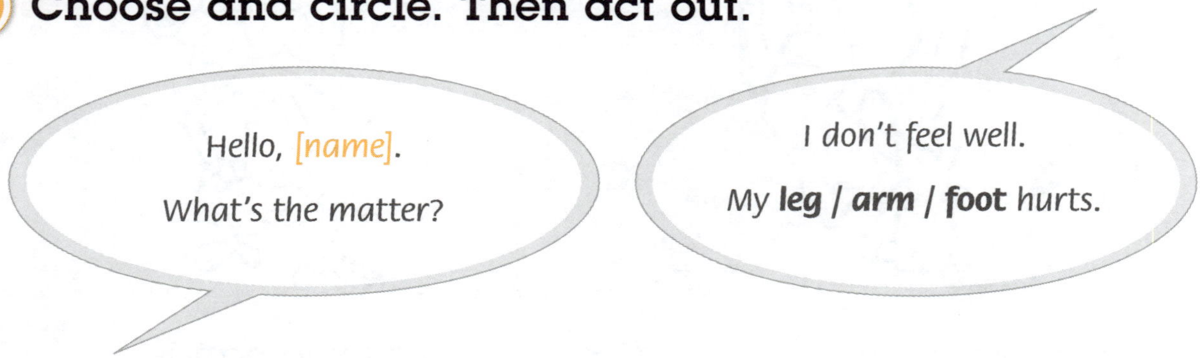

2 **Read the story in your Student Book. Write J (Jake) or D (Doodle).**

1 He's small and green. D
2 He has two eyes. ☐
3 He has short legs. ☐
4 He has one eye. ☐

3 **What happens next? Draw.**

1 Complete.

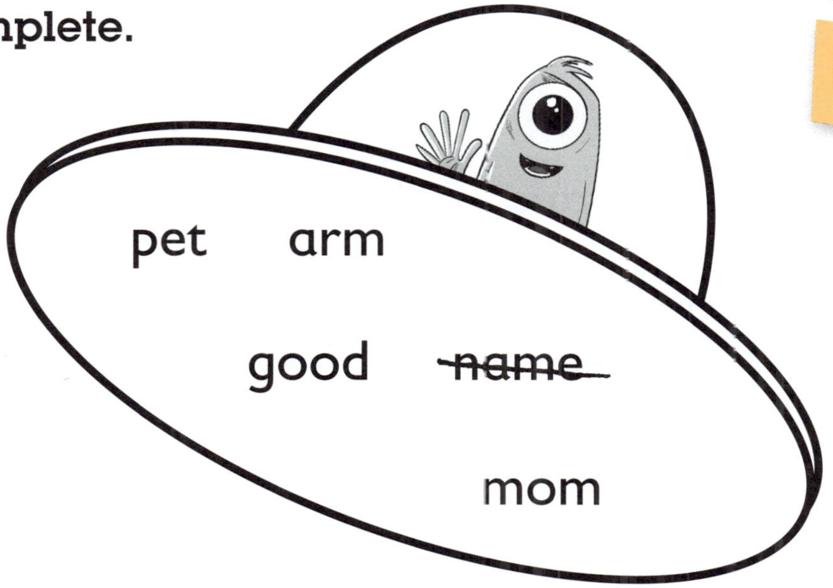

1 What's your ....name.... ?

2 I'm not your ....

3 Jake has a funny ....

4 My .... hurts.

5 You're a .... friend.

2 Complete with "." or "!".

I Can Read!

1 Ouch ..!..

2 He's my friend ....

3 Don't go ....

4 My hand hurts ....

5 Look ....

6 It has short arms ....

3 Do you like the story? Choose and circle.

Yes! 🙂 No. 🙁 I'm not sure. 😐

Lesson 5

1 What's missing? Draw and write.

1

ears

2

3

4

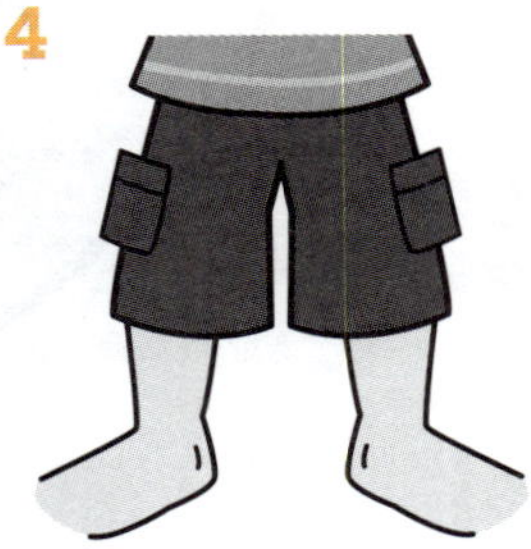

2 Match. Then say more words in each category.

red six short four blue eyes legs big

parts of the body ***colors*** ***numbers*** ***other adjectives***

feet two head black nine arms yellow face

3 Say the words. Circle *a* as it sounds in *face*.

a

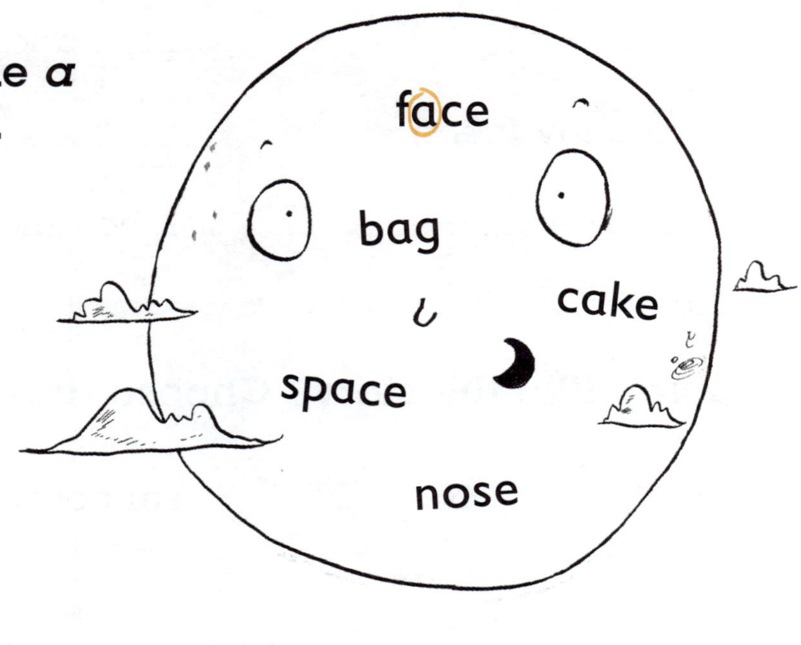

1 Look and write descriptions.

He has	He doesn't have	She has	She doesn't have

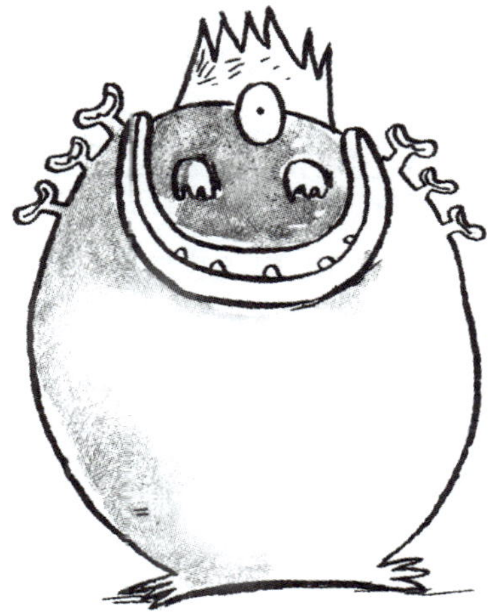

1 She has three eyes.
2 ______ long hair.
3 ______ eight toes.
4 He has six ears.
5 ______ any arms.
6 ______ one mouth.

2 Draw a monster. Answer the questions.

How many . . .

ears does it have?

It has ______.

feet does it have?

______.

noses does it have?

______.

toes does it have?

______.

Lesson 7

CLIL

1 Read and circle T (true) or F (false).

1 Mars has one moon. T / F

2 Venus is next to Mercury. T / F

3 The sun is a star. T / F

4 Earth is the third planet from the sun. T / F

5 Jupiter is very small. T / F

6 Neptune has rings. T / F

2 Use your Student Book research. Write a quiz. Ask and answer.

Find Out More!

Planet Quiz Team Name ....

1 ....

2 ....

3 ....

4 ....

5 ....

1 Find and circle six differences. Then write.

A

B

It has five ears. — It has ________.

It has ________. — It has ________.

It doesn't have ________. — It doesn't have ________.

2 Talk to a friend.

Chapter 8 I Like Food!

Lesson 1

1 Number.

pizza	2	burger		broccoli	
chicken		fries		peas	
pasta		green beans		salad	
				fish	

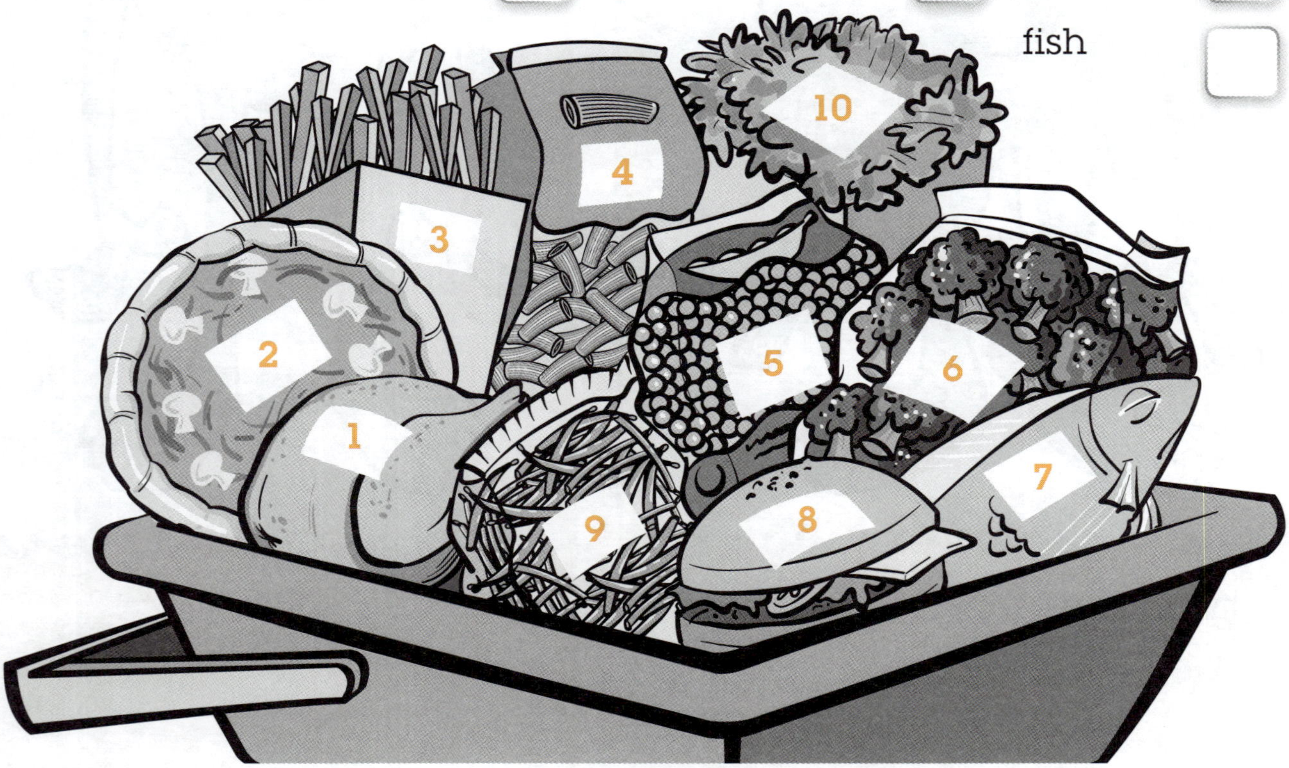

2 Write the words from Activity 1 in two groups.

I like this food.	I don't like this food.

1 Look, read, and circle.

1
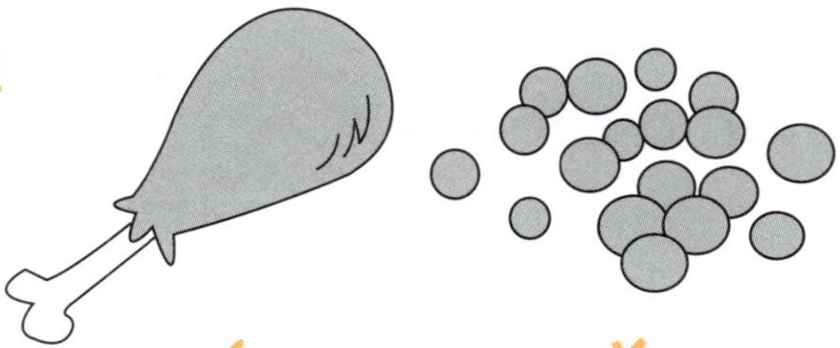
✔ ✘

2
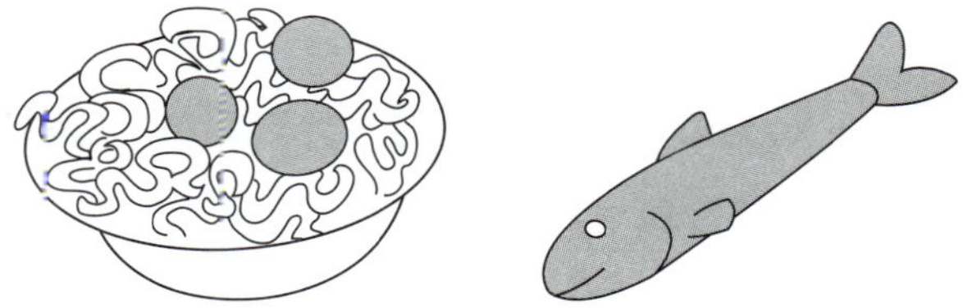
✔ ✘

3
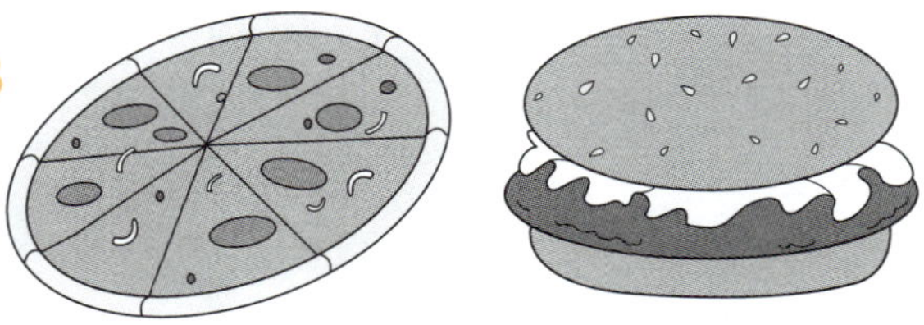
✘ ✔

4
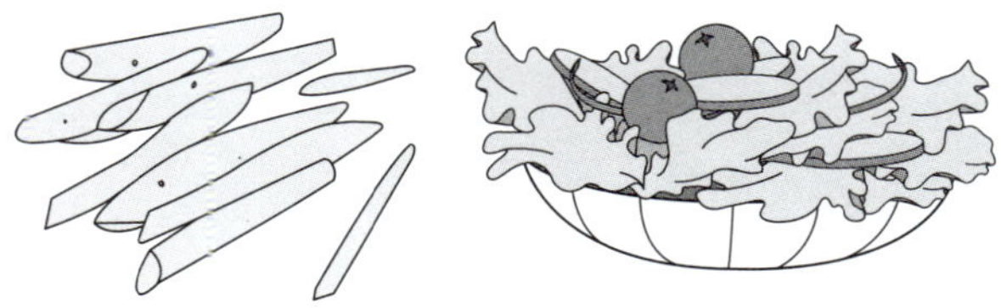
✔ ✘

1 I **like** / **don't like** chicken, but I **like** / **don't like** peas.

2 I **like** / **don't like** pasta, but I **like** / **don't like** fish.

3 I **like** / **don't like** pizza, but I **like** / **don't like** burgers.

4 I **like** / **don't like** fries, but I **like** / **don't like** salad.

2 Write sentences about foods you like and don't like.

1 I like ...., but I don't like ....

2 I like ....

3 ....

3 Now talk to a friend.

I like peas, but I don't like green beans.

Lesson 3

1 **Choose and circle. Complete the dialogue. Then act out.**

I like this **story / color / animal**, [name].

Hmm, sorry, I don't. I like this **story / color / animal**.

Oh! Me, too!

2 **Read the story in your Student Book. Complete for Chip.**

1 I ....like.... pizza, but ....I don't like.... salad.

2 I like chicken, ... green beans.

3 .... cake.

3 **What happens next? Choose and check (✔).**

Lesson 4
Time to Think

1 **Color the food. Then write the words in the correct place.**

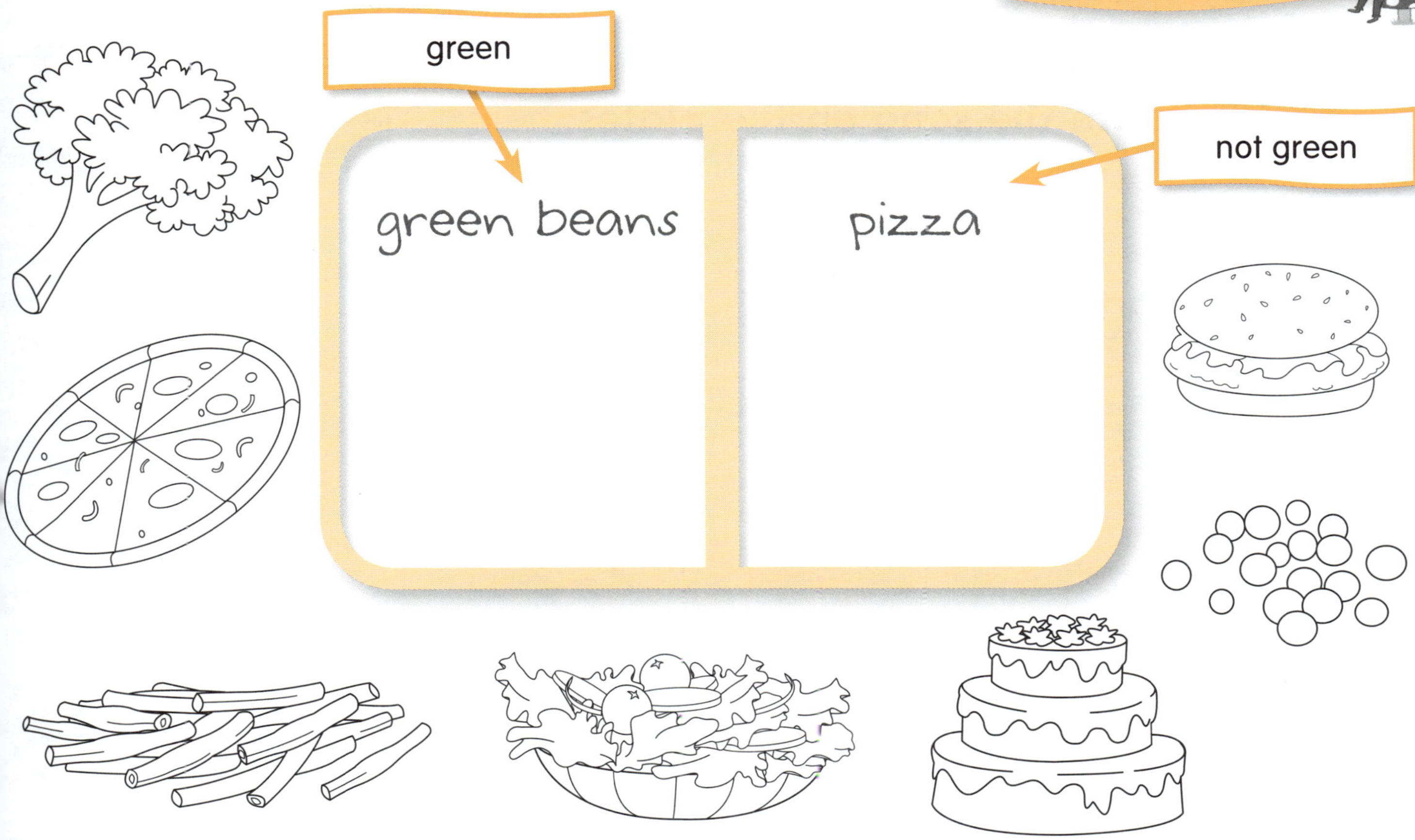

2 **Complete with “ ”.**

1 “Do you have any cake?” asks Chip.

2 No, I don't, says Chip.

3 Pizza, please, says Chip.

4 Is there any cake? asks Chip.

3 **Do you like the story? Choose and circle.**

Yes!  No.  I'm not sure. 

Lesson 5

ice cream	cheese
cake	~~salad~~
chicken	rice
pizza	pasta

1 **Complete the words. Then write the food from the song on the plates.**

M o nday — salad

Tues _ _ _

_ _ dn _ _ day

T _ _ _ _ day

_ ri _ _ _

S _ t _ _ day

S _ _ day

2 **Now say for you.**

On Friday I have rice!

3 **Say the words. Circle *ee* or *ea* as it sounds in *cheese*. Underline *i* as it sounds in *chicken*.**

1 Complete the menu.

LUNCH MENU

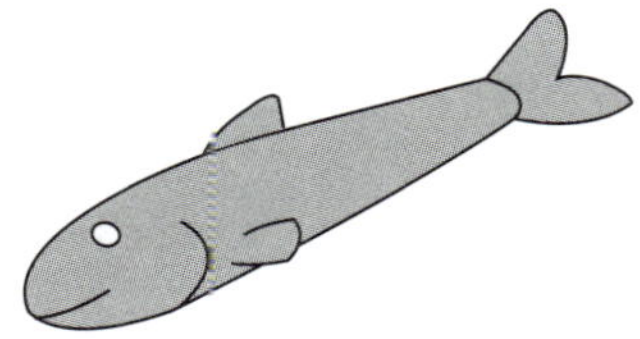

burger .... OR ....

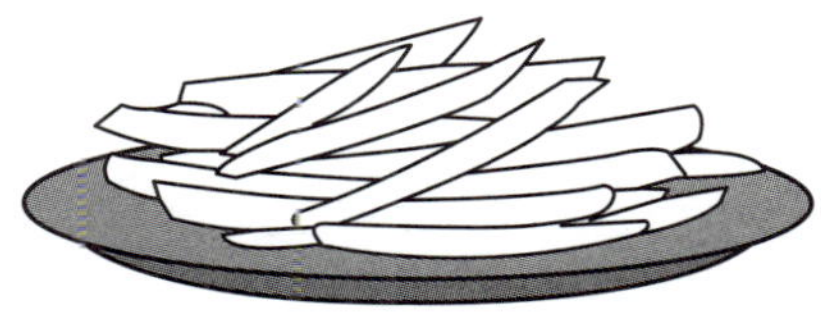

.... OR ....

.... OR ....

2 Look at the menu in Activity 1. Complete the questions. Then circle your answers.

1 Do you like burgers? **Yes, I do. / No, I don't.**

2 .... you like fish? **Yes, I do. / No, I don't.**

3 .... you .... salad? **Yes, I do. / No, I don't.**

4 Do .... ice cream? **Yes, I do. / No, I don't.**

Lesson 7

CLIL

1 Write your food blog for today.

MY FOOD BLOG

Today is ....

Lunch today is ....

I like ....

.... is healthy.

.... isn't very healthy.

2 Ask a friend about their lunch.

What's your lunch today?

Is it healthy?

3 Use your Student Book research. Write and draw a Healthy Food Leaflet.

Find Out More!

Eat Healthy Food

1	2	3

1 **Ask and answer with a friend.**

Quiz

How healthy are you?

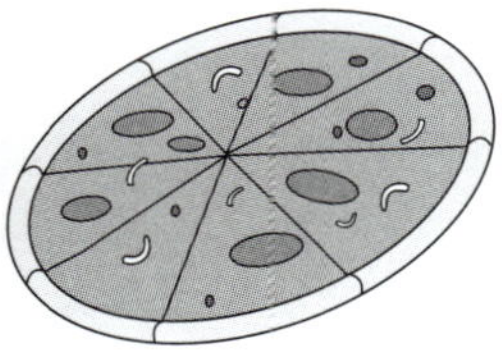

1 Do you like pizza?
Yes, I do.
No, I don't.

2 Do you have cake for lunch?
Yes, I do.
No, I don't.

3 Do you have fruit every day?
Yes, I do.
No, I don't.

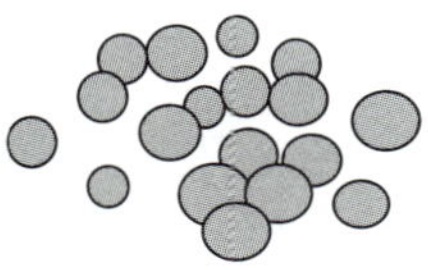

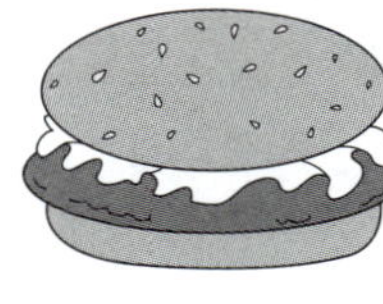

4 Do you like fish?
Yes, I do.
No, I don't.

5 Do you have salad, broccoli, green beans, or peas every day?
Yes, I do.
No, I don't.

6 Do you sometimes have fries for lunch?
Yes, I do.
No, I don't.

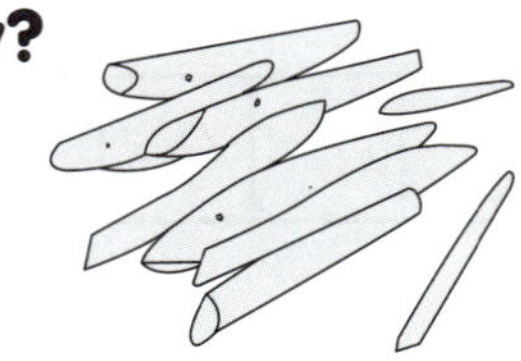

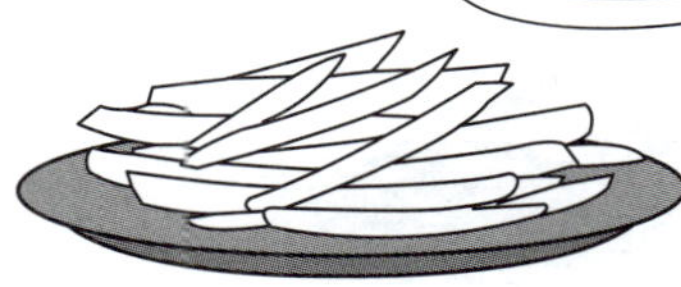

Figure out your score:

1
Yes = 1
No = 2

3
Yes = 3
No = 1

5
Yes = 3
No = 1

2
Yes = 1
No = 2

4
Yes = 2
No = 1

6
Yes = 1
No = 2

Read your results:

6–9 Some foods are bad for you. Don't eat unhealthy food every day. Eat more fruit and vegetables.

10–14 Good work! You're healthy. You like fruit and vegetables. You eat lots of healthy food.

Chapter 9 Sports and Music

Lesson 1

1 Complete the puzzle.

2 Write the words in two groups.

I like to do this.	I don't like to do this.

play soccer
ride a bike
run
skate
dance
swim

Lesson 2

1 Look and complete.

can
He
She
It
can't

1 She can run.
2 .... play soccer.
3 .... ride a bike.
4 .... skate.
5 .... dance.
6 .... swim.

2 Complete the questions and circle your answers.

1 Can you skate? **Yes, I can. / No, I can't.**
2 .... swim? **Yes, I can. / No, I can't.**
3 .... ride a bike? **Yes, I can. / No, I can't.**

3 Write two more questions. Ask a friend and write his/her answers.

1 Can you .... ? ....
2 .... ? ....

Lesson 3

1 Choose and write. Then circle and act out.

Look at this

------------------------------.

It's magic.

It's **true!** / **Look!**

Don't be silly! / That's funny! / No, it isn't!

2 Read the story in your Student Book. Circle.

My name's Tim.

1 I **can** / **can't** play the violin.

2 I **can** / **can't** drive a cart.

3 I **can** / **can't** sing.

4 Fish **can** / **can't** fly when I play my violin.

3 What happens when Tim plays his violin? Choose an animal and draw.

1 What happens in the story? Write sentences.

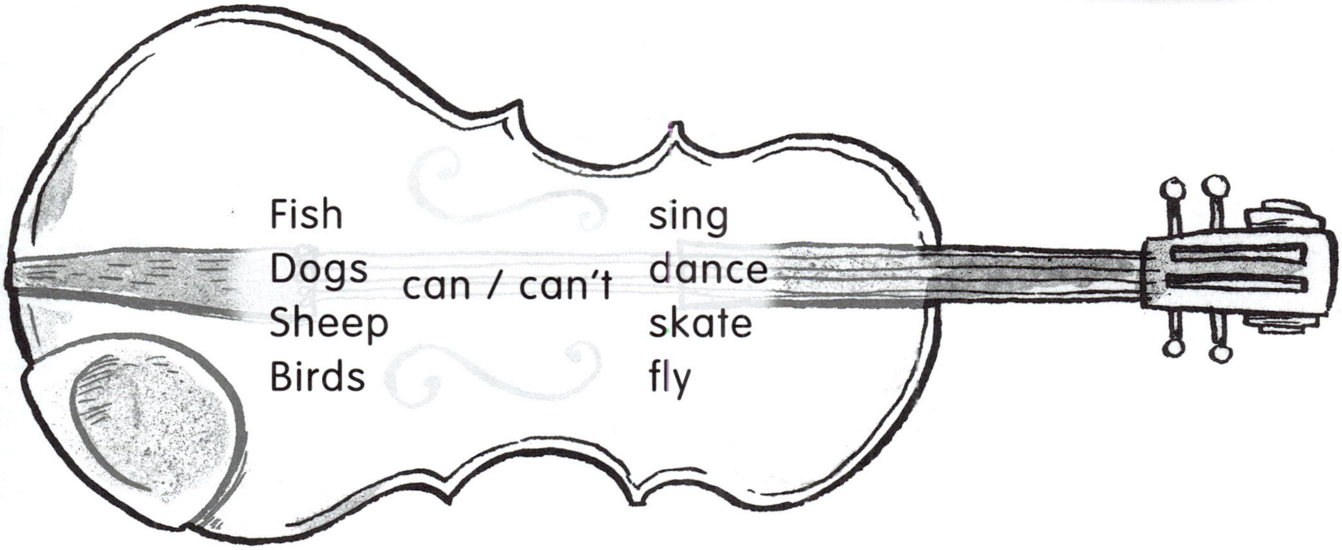

1 Fish can fly.

2 ______________________ .

3 ______________________ .

4 ______________________ .

2 Match the words that rhyme.

I Can Read!

Tim	boy	man	tree	play	run
say	three	violin	toy	fun	van

3 Do you like the story? Choose and circle.

Yes! ☺ No. ☹ I'm not sure. 😐

Lesson 5

1 **Circle six words for musical instruments.**

2 **Look and write the instruments in the correct column for you.**

Can you play the …?

Yes, I can.	No, I can't.

3 **Say the words. Circle *a* as it sounds in *bang*. Underline *u* as it sounds in *drum*.**

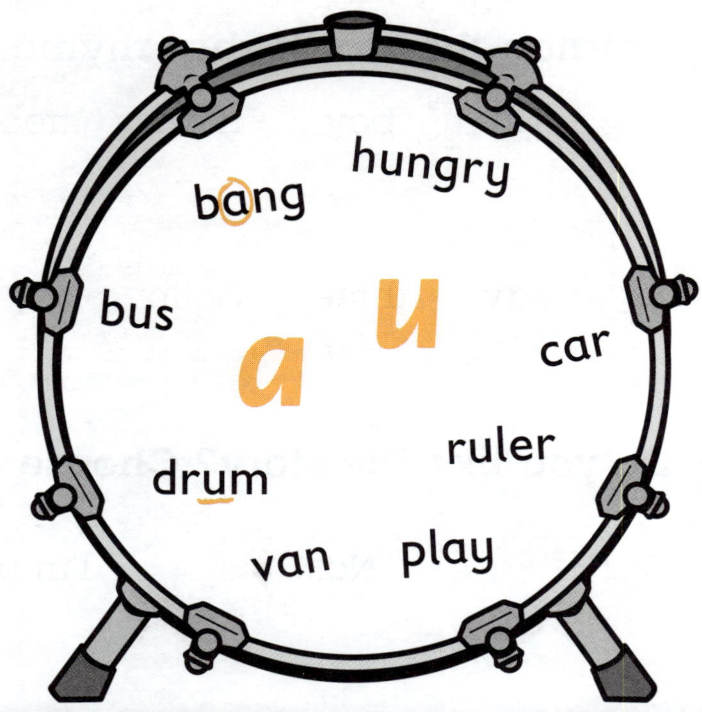

1 Look. Complete the questions and write the answers.

Yes, he can.
No, she can't.
~~No, he can't.~~
Yes, she can.

1 Can he play the drums? No, he can't.

2 .... play the tambourine? ....

3 .... play the violin? ....

4 .... play the recorder? ....

2 Complete the Talent Show poster for a friend. Choose two things he/she can do.

Talent Show

On ....

At ....

He / She can

....

....

....

Lesson 7
CLIL

1 **Read and circle *tuba* or *bouzouki*.**

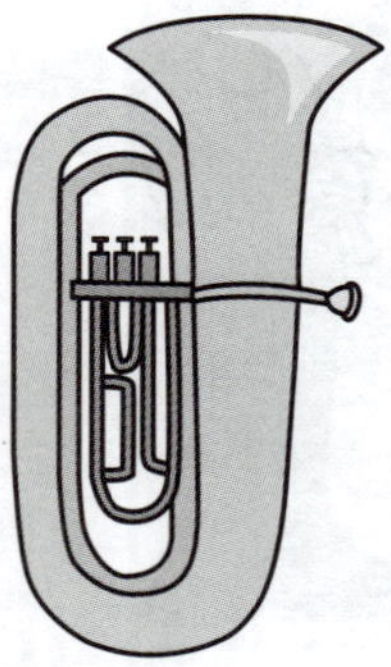

This instrument is
from Germany.
It's called a tuba.
It isn't small. It's very big.
You play it with your
mouth and hands.

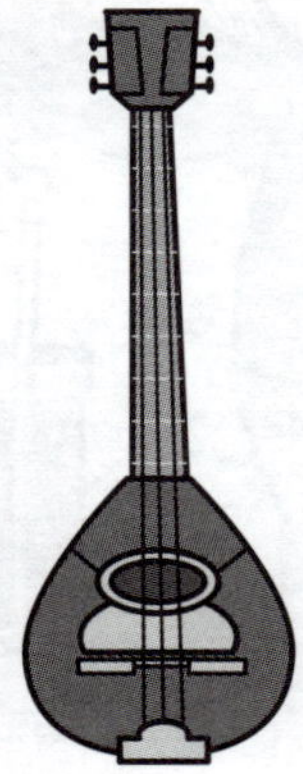

This instrument is
from Greece.
It's called a bouzouki.
It isn't very big. It's small.
You play it with your
hands.

1 It isn't small. **(tuba)** / **bouzouki**

2 It's from Germany. **tuba** / **bouzouki**

3 It's from Greece. **tuba** / **bouzouki**

4 You don't play it with your mouth. **tuba** / **bouzouki**

2 **Use your Student Book research. Complete for drums and piano. Then draw another instrument and complete.**

Find Out More!

	hands	feet	mouth
	✔		

1 **Play the game. Roll the dice. Ask and answer.**

Can you skate?

Yes, I can. / No, I can't.

Chapter 1 Exam Booster

1 Reading and Writing
Look and read. Put a tick ✓ or cross ✗ in the box. There are two examples.

Examples

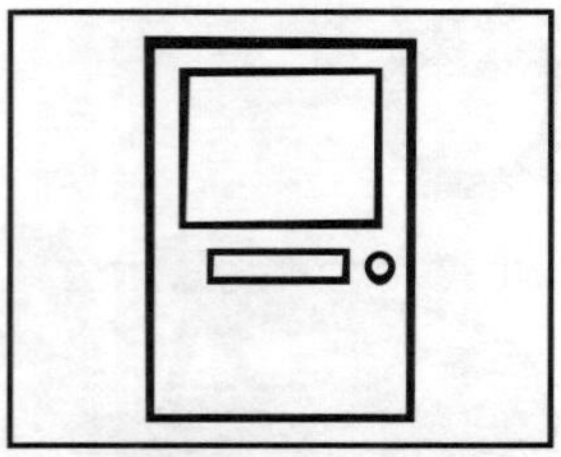

It's a door. ✓

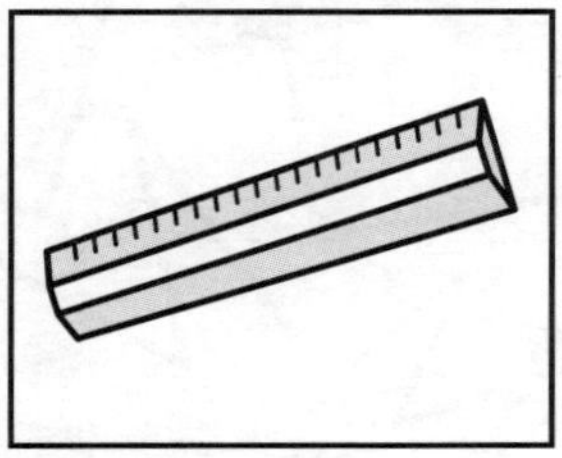

It's a pencil case. ✗

Questions

1

It's a notebook. ☐

2

It's an eraser. ☐

3

It's a table. ☐

4

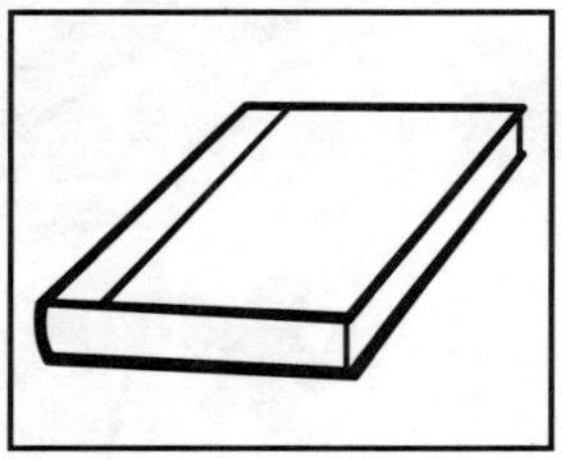

It's a book. ☐

5

It's a bag. ☐

2 Listening

Listen and color. There is one example.

3 Reading and Writing

Look and read. Put a tick ✓ or cross ✗ in the box. There are two examples.

Examples

It's a bag. ✓

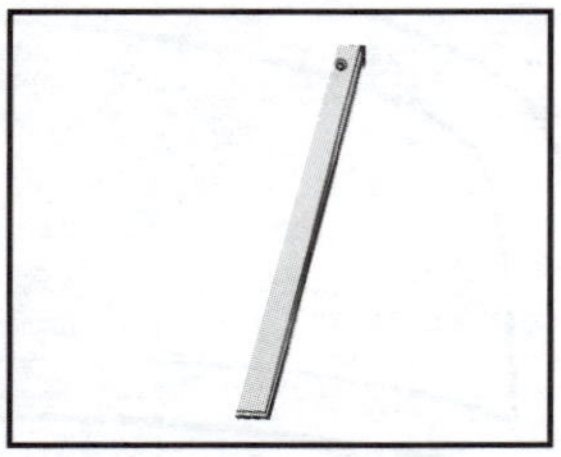

It's a pen. ✗

Questions

1 

It's an orange book. ☐

2 

It's a tree. ☐

3 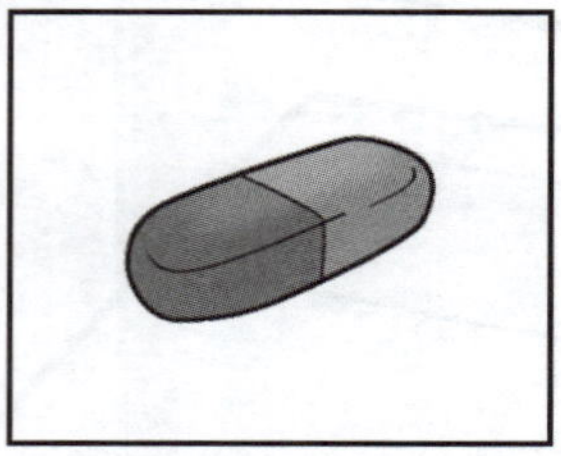

It's an eraser. ☐

4 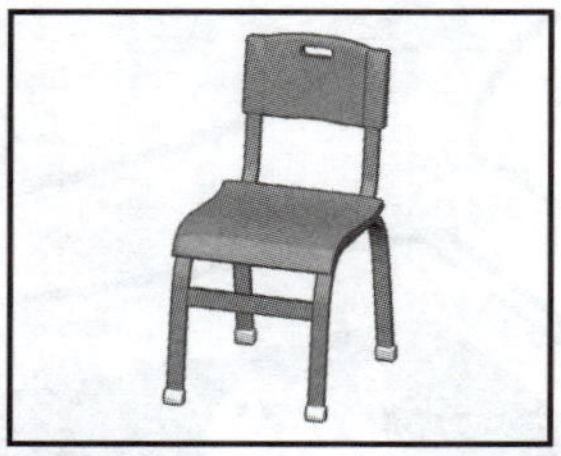

It's a table. ☐

5 

It's an orange crayon. ☐

Exam Tip

Use a pencil and an eraser so you can change your answers.

1 Reading and Writing
Look at the letters. Write the words.

Example

J a n u a r y

Questions

1 _ _ _ _ _

2 _ _ _ _

3 _ _ _ _ _ _

4 _ _ _ _ _ _ _ _ _

5 _ _ _ _ _ _ _ _

2 Listening

Listen and tick ✓ the box. There is one example.

Example Which toy is Tom's?

a

b
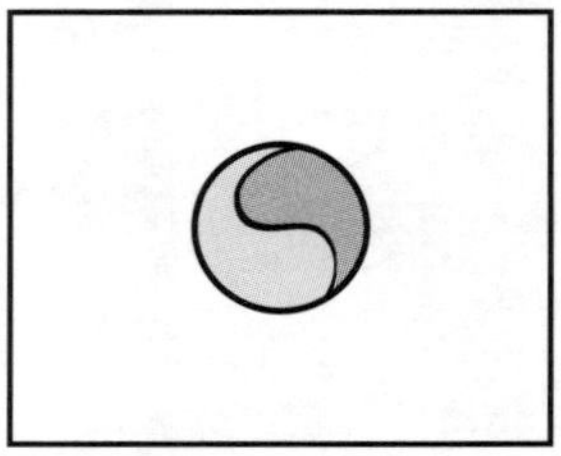

c

✓

Questions

1 When's Anna's birthday?

a

b

c

2 Which is Kim's favorite toy?

a

b

c

3 How old is Max?

a

b

c

3 Listening

Listen and tick ✓ the box. There is one example.

Example What's Adam's favorite toy?

a  ☐

b  ☑

c  ☐

Questions

1 Which card is for Lucy?

a 

☐

b 

☐

c 

☐

2 What's Tony's new toy?

a 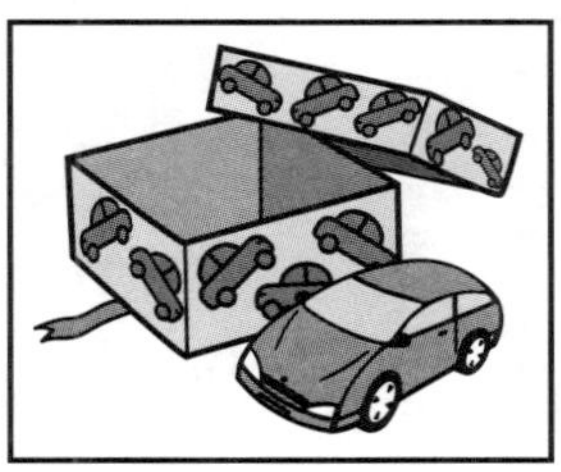 ☐

b  ☐

c  ☐

3 Which is Grace's bag?

a  ☐

b  ☐

c  ☐

Exam Tip

Look at the pictures first.
Listen carefully.

Chapter 3 Exam Booster

1 Reading and Writing
Read this. Choose a word from the picture. Write the correct word next to numbers 1–5. There is one example.

This animal is orange, black, and white. It's a tiger.

This animal is very tall. It's a (**1**) ....

This animal is scary. It's a (**2**) ....

This animal is very big. It's an (**3**) ....

This animal is hungry. It's a (**4**) ....

This animal is small and it's in a tree. It's a (**5**) ....

2 Listening

Listen and tick ✓ the box. There is one example.

Example Which animals are they?

a  ☐

b  ☑

c  ☐

Questions

1 Which animals are they?

a  ☐

b  ☐

c  ☐

2 Which animals are they?

a  ☐

b  ☐

c  ☐

3 Which animal is it?

a  ☐

b  ☐

c  ☐

3 Speaking

1 Read and listen. Tick ✓ the sentences you hear. There is one example.

What's this? ☐	Are crocodiles green? ☐
What are these? ✓	Tell me about giraffes. ☐
Are tigers scary? ☐	What's your favorite animal? ☐

2 Talk about the picture with a partner. Use the examples from Activity 1.

3 Now listen and compare. Find two facts about each animal.

Exam Tip

It's OK to say, "Sorry, I don't know."

Chapter 4 Exam Booster

1 Reading and Writing

Look at the picture and read the questions. Write one-word answers.

Example

Where's the boy? under the ___table___

Questions

1 What's on the desk? a ______

2 Where's the spider? on the ______

3 Where's the bag? in the ______

4 Where's the monkey? ______ the chair

5 Where's the teddy bear? ______ the shelf

2 Listening

Listen and draw lines. There is one example.

Tom Pat Bill

May Alan Dan Lucy

3 Reading and Writing

Look at the picture and read the questions. Write one-word answers.

Examples

Where's the piano?	behind the ...sofa...
How many doors are there?	...two...

Questions

1	Which room are they in?	the .... room
2	Where's the boy?	.... the sofa
3	How many TVs are there?	....
4	Where's the tree?	in the ....
5	What color is the sofa?	....

Exam Tip

Remember to write only one word for each answer.

Chapter 5 Exam Booster

1 Reading and Writing

Look and read. Write *yes* or *no*.

Examples

The library is across from the café. yes

There's a movie theater. no

Questions

1 The swimming pool is next to the park. ....

2 There's a hotel. ....

3 The zoo is across from the school. ....

4 There are two cafés. ....

5 The school is next to the swimming pool. ....

2 Listening

Listen and color. There is one example.

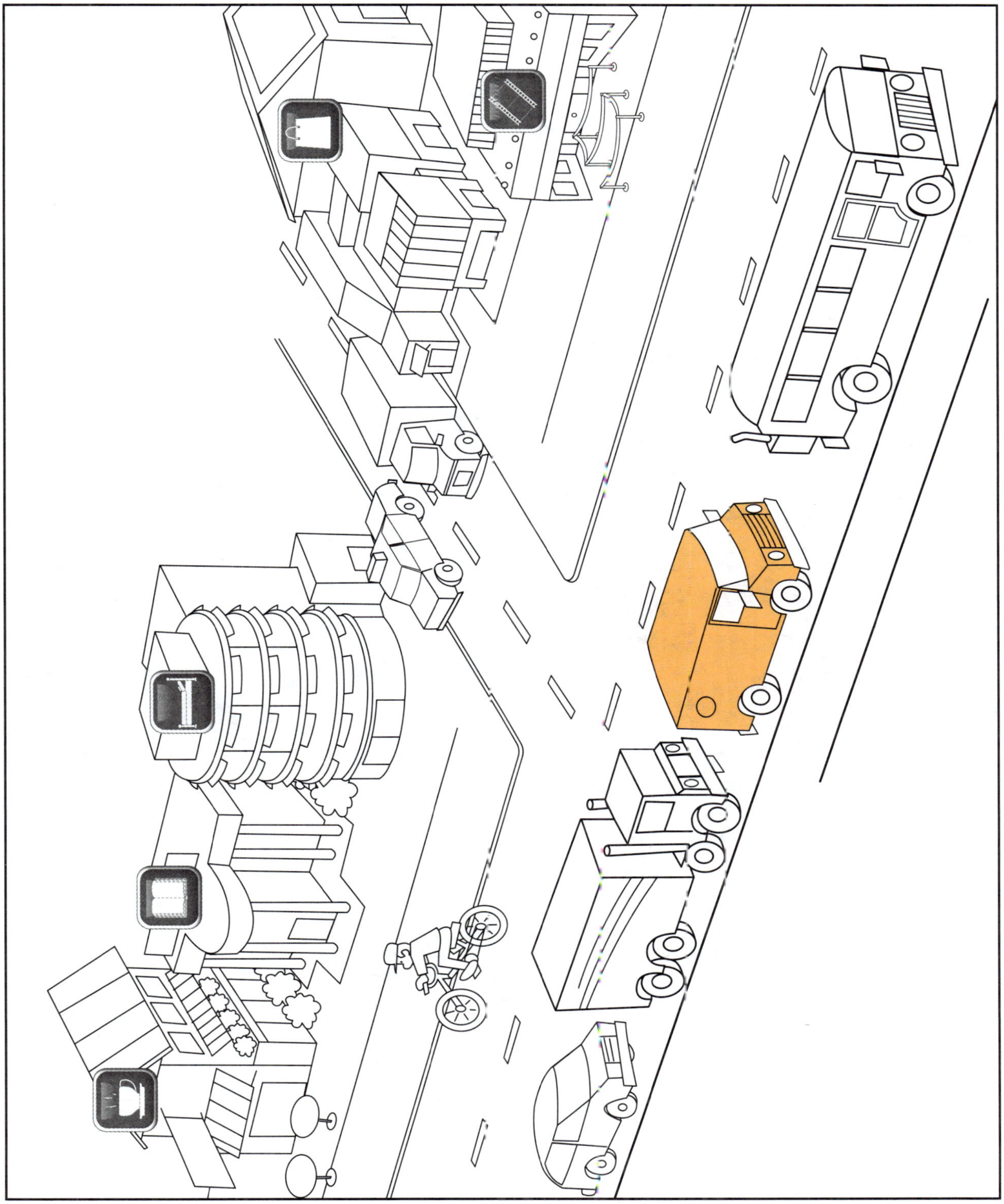

3 Listening

Listen and color. There is one example.

Exam Tip

Listen carefully for the objects and the colors.

Chapter 6 Exam Booster

1 Reading and Writing

Look and read. Write *yes* or *no*.

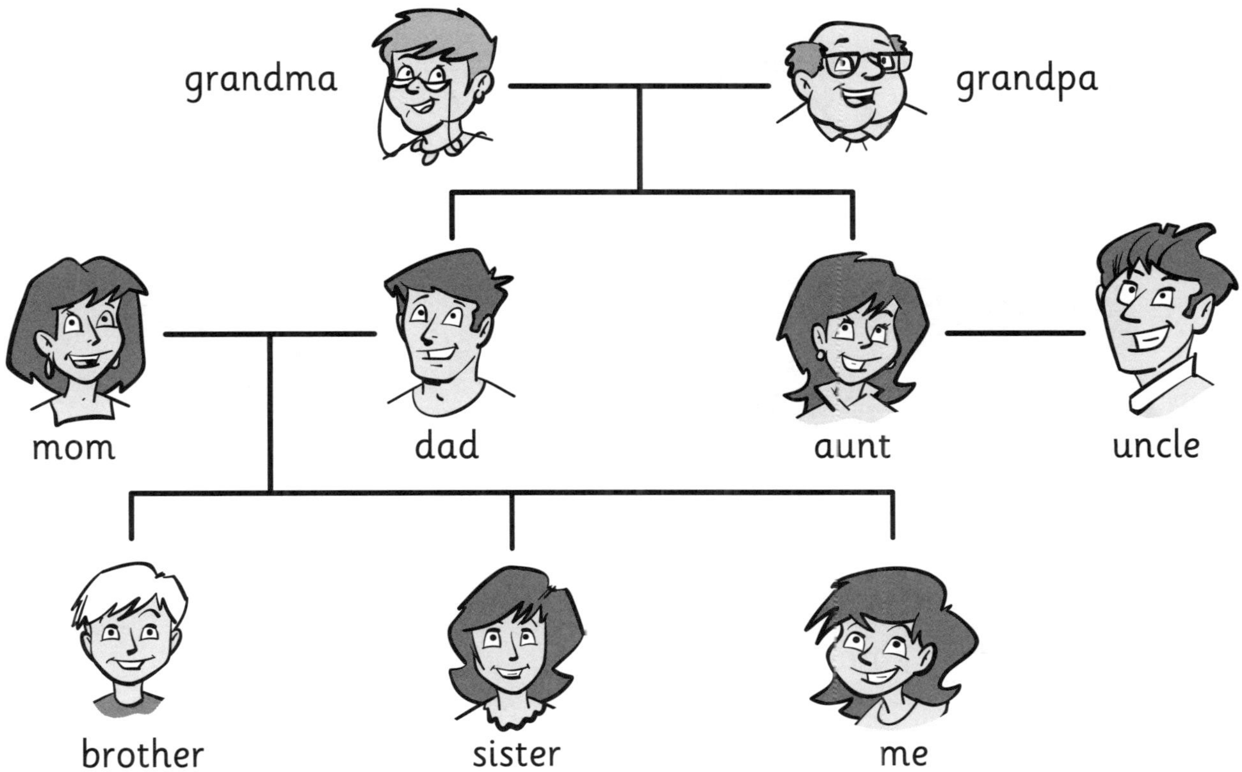

Examples

This is my mom. yes

I don't have a grandpa. no

Questions

1 I have three brothers. ....

2 I don't have any aunts or uncles. ....

3 I have a grandma. ....

4  This is my dad. ....

5 I have a sister. ....

2 Listening

🔊 Read the question. Listen and write a name or a number. There are two examples.

Examples

What's Pat's sister's name? Kim

How old is her sister? five

Questions

1 How old is Pat? ....

2 How many aunts does she have? ....

3 How old is her brother? ....

4 What's her grandma's name? ....

5 How old is Tom? ....

3 Speaking

1 Look and listen to the example. Complete the questions.

1 .... is she?

2 When's .... ?

2 Match the questions with the pictures.

1 Which pets does the girl have?
What's your favorite pet?

2 How many sisters does the boy have?
Do you have a brother or sister?

3 Is there a swimming pool in your town?
Can you swim?

4 What are these?
What's your favorite animal?

a 

b 

c 

d 

3 Choose two pictures. Ask and answer the questions with a friend.

4 Now listen and compare. Are your answers the same or different?

Exam Tip

If you can't hear or don't understand the question, say, "Can you repeat the question, please?"

Chapter 7 Exam Booster

1 Reading and Writing
Read this. Choose a word from the box. Write the correct word next to numbers 1–5. There is one example.

A Dinosaur

It doesn't have any ......arms...... . It has four (**1**) ....

It has two (**2**) .... It has a long (**3**) ....

It has a big (**4**) .... It has a short (**5**) ....

Examples

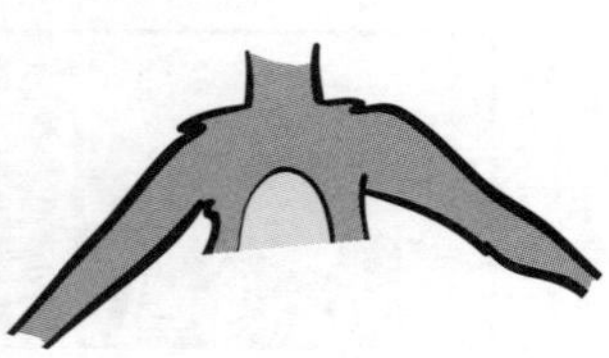

~~arms~~

tail

hair

neck

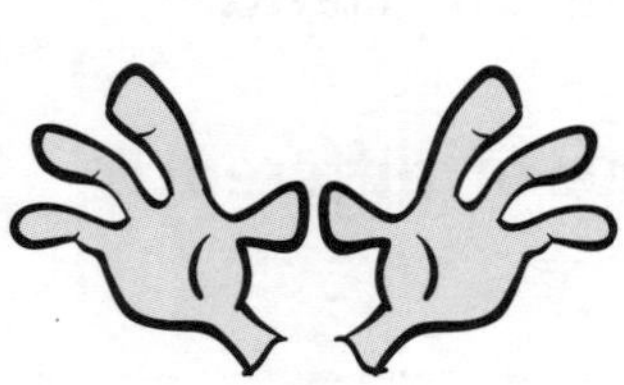

hands

head

legs

eyes

2 Listening

🔊 Read the question. Listen and write a name or a number. There are two examples.

Examples

What's the boy's name? ....Sam........

How old is the boy? ....eight........

Questions

1 What's Sam's friend's name? ....

2 How many legs does the monster have? ....

3 How many elephants are there? ....

4 Who draws lions and tigers? ....

5 How many eyes does the alien have? ....

3 Reading and Writing

Read this. Choose a word from the box. Write the correct word next to numbers 1–5. There is one example.

A Pet Hamster

A hamster is a great pet. It has a small head, four short legs, and four little (**1**) .... Can you see a tail? A hamster doesn't have a long (**2**) .... It has a cute (**3**) .... with two eyes and two pink (**4**) .... Hamsters don't need a lot of space. You don't need a big (**5**) .... to have a hamster.

Example

~~hamster~~

tail

feet

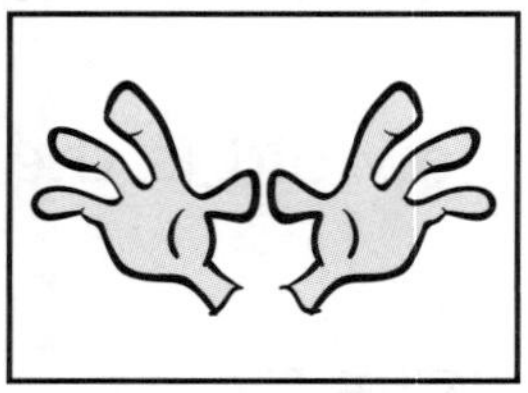

hands

yard

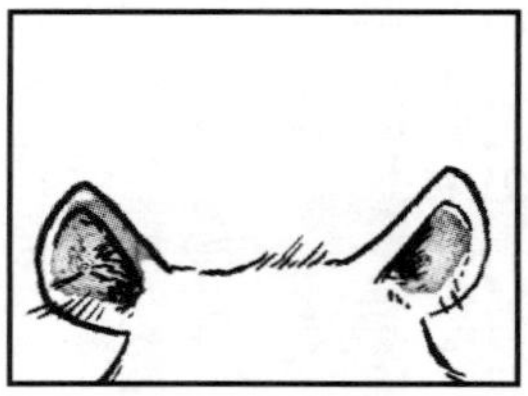

ears

face

rat

Exam Tip

Read all the sentences before you choose the words.

Chapter 8 Exam Booster

1 Reading and Writing

Look and read. Write *yes* or *no*.

Monday		Friday	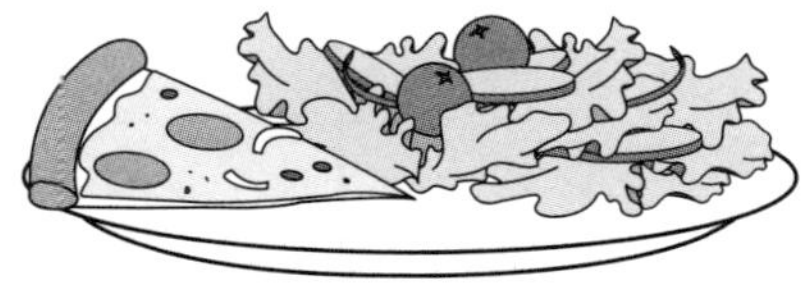
Tuesday		Saturday	
Wednesday	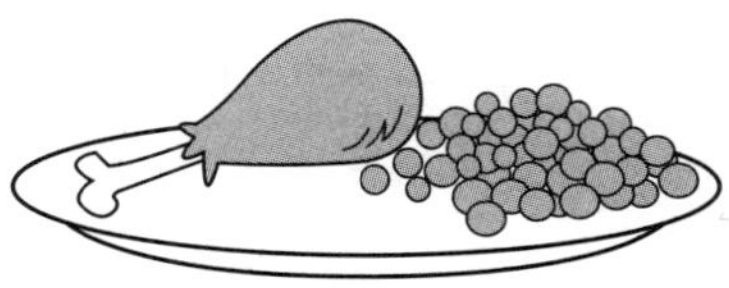	Sunday	
Thursday	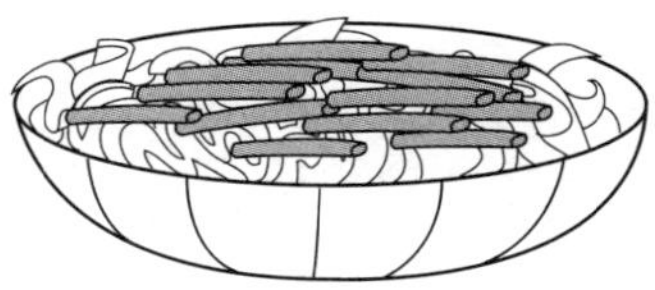		

Examples

On Monday, I have pasta. yes

On Saturday, I have chicken and fries. no

Questions

1 On Wednesday, I have chicken and broccoli. ....

2 On Friday, I have pizza and salad. ....

3 On Sunday, I have burger and fries. ....

4 On Tuesday, I have fish and green beans. ....

5 On Thursday, I have pasta and green beans. ....

2 Listening

Listen and draw lines. There is one example.

Ann Sarah Grace

Sue Tony Sam Danny

3 Listening

Listen and draw lines. There is one example.

Frank Lucy Dan

Lucas Jill Alex Ben

Exam Tip

Draw the lines using a pencil and use an eraser if you change your mind.

Chapter 9 Exam Booster

1 Reading and Writing

Look at the pictures. Look at the letters. Write the words.

Example

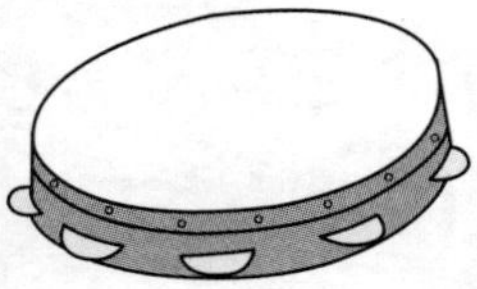

t a m b o u r i n e

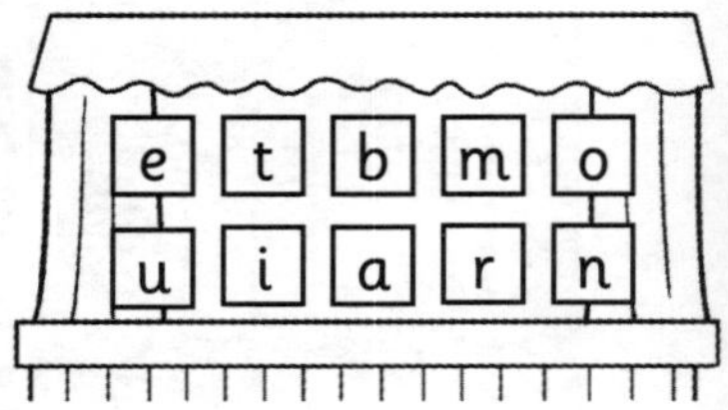

Questions

1 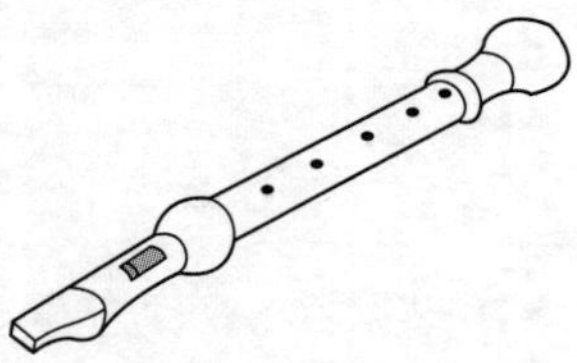

_ _ _ _ _ _ _ _

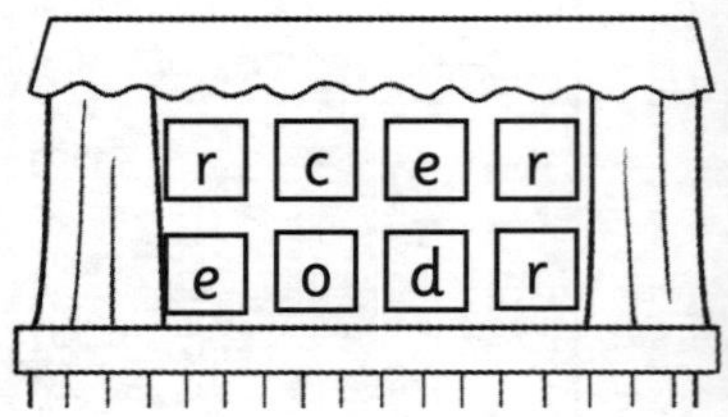

2 

_ _ _ _ _ _

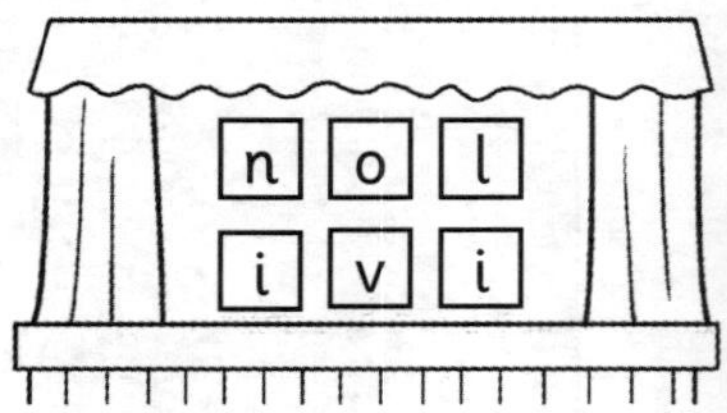

3 

_ _ _ _ _ _

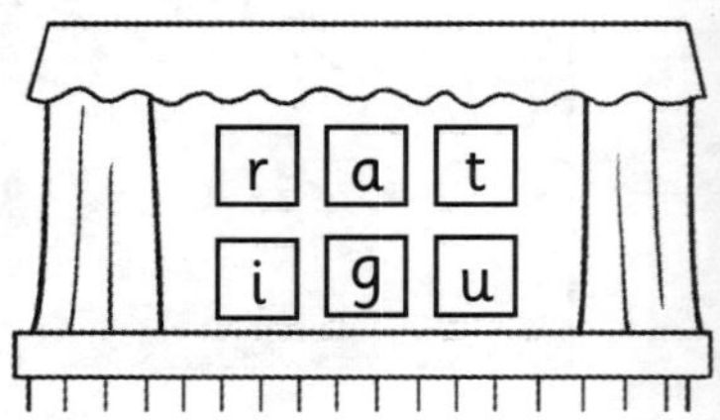

4 

_ _ _ _ _

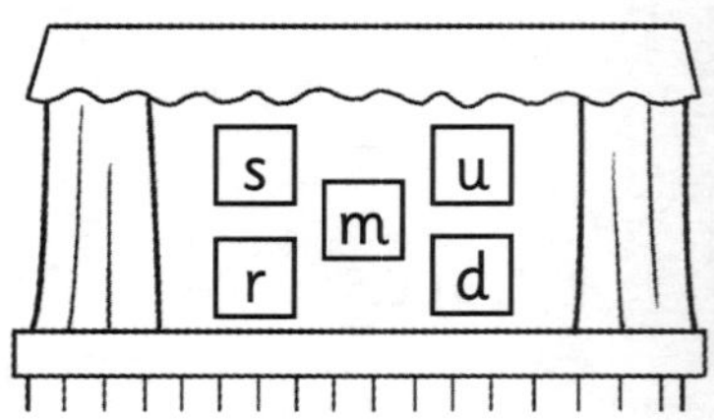

5 

_ _ _ _ _

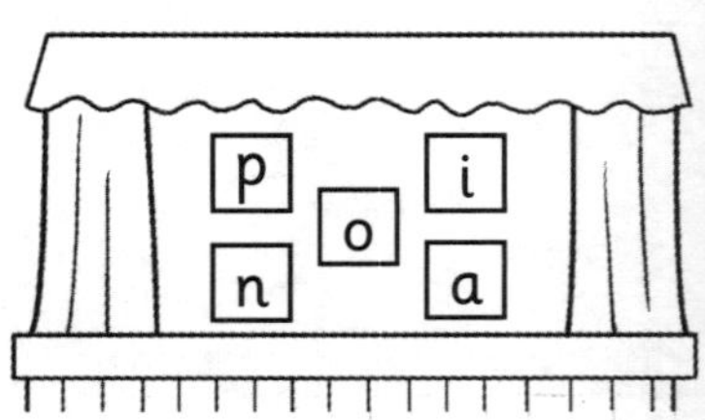

2 Listening

🔊 **Listen and tick ✓ the box. There is one example.**

Example What can Bill do?

a  ☑

b  ☐

c  ☐

Questions

1 Which instrument can Sue play?

a  ☐

b 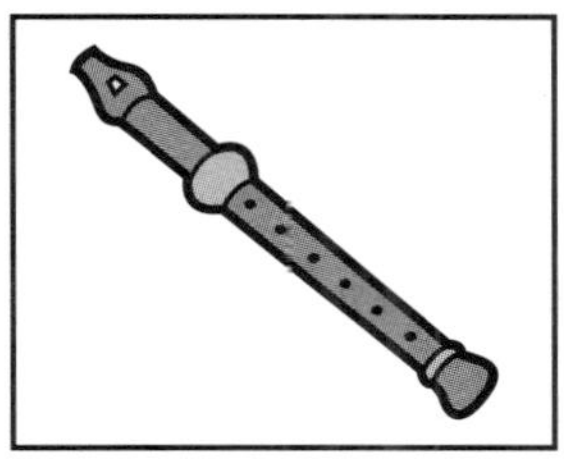 ☐

c  ☐

2 Which is Anna's favorite sport?

a  ☐

b  ☐

c  ☐

3 Which is Katie's favorite animal?

a  ☐

b  ☐

c  ☐

3 Speaking

1 Look and listen to the example. Circle the correct words.

Can you see the **guitar** / **teddy bear** / **cat**?

Put the teddy bear **in** / **on** / **under** the **sofa** / **shelf** / **box**.

2 In pairs, take turns to talk about your picture. Listen and draw lines.

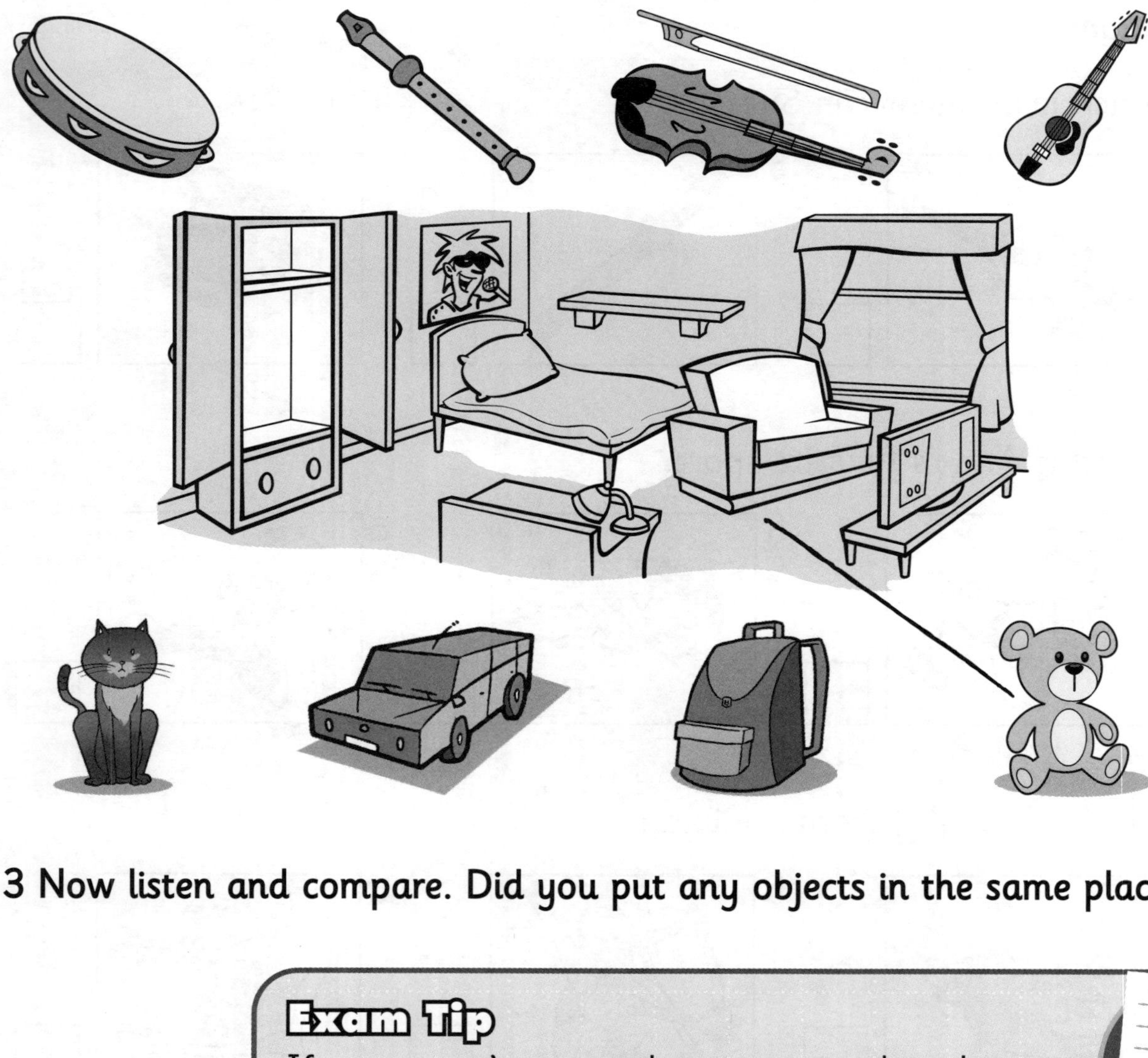

3 Now listen and compare. Did you put any objects in the same place?

Exam Tip
If you aren't sure where to put the objects, ask, "Is it next to the ...?" or "Where is it?"

Story Central Reader 1

Contents

Chapter 1

Chen's Magic Pen

7
Wow!
It's a tree.
8
It's a horse.
A brown horse!
Thank you, Chen.
Thank you.
9
What is it, Mama?
Rice! Look!
It's rice – beautiful, white rice.
10
Gold, please!
No.
What!
No gold?

11
Ha!
Aaargh! Help!
12
Hmm.
13
Look, it's a door. Ha-ha!
14
Aaargh! It isn't a magic pen.

The Princess and the Teddy Bear

Chapter 2

4
My teddy bear is my favorite toy!
Oh, Polly! How old are you?
I'm 13.
5
Here's a teddy bear.
That isn't my teddy bear. My teddy bear is yellow.
6
Look at this teddy bear.
That isn't my teddy bear. My teddy bear is small.
7
Please help...
8
Please help Princess Polly. Find my teddy bear. It's small and yellow.
9
Oh! This teddy bear is small and yellow.

10
Is this your teddy bear?
Yes, it is. Thank you.
11
Wait. When's your birthday?
It's in June.
Happy Birthday! This is your teddy bear now.
Oh. Thank you, Princess Polly!
12

Chapter 3

The Hungry Giraffe

7
Whooaaa! My neck!
8
Mmm! These leaves aren't brown. They're green.
9
Thank you!
10
Here! Eat these. I'm not hungry at all.
Thank you, Giraffe.

Chapter 4 THE MYSTERY HOUSE

4
Can I come? Pleeeeease?
No!
Uh... Yes, of course. Find the cat. Look in that big old house.
It's scary. Hmm, where's the cat? It's small and black.
What's that?
5
6
Oh, it's a cat. Come here, Kitty.
7
Hello? Can I come in?
8
It's behind the door. It's in the living room.
9
Hmm, is it under the table? No.
10
It isn't in the kitchen.

11
Aha! A clue.
12
It's in the bedroom.
13
Oh, you're on the chair! Come here.
Meow!
14
Aargh! Help. Go away!

15
Oh, what's on the shelf? It's the necklace!
16
Sit down on the chair, Kitty! Don't move.
17
Whoa, I'm on the chair, and it's scary.
18
Hello, Mrs. Ruiz. Is this your cat?
Oh, yes, it's my Kitty! Thank you.
19
And look – the necklace.
Wow!
20
Here – Welcome to The Mystery Club!
Thanks!
I ♥ Mystery

Chapter 5

Captain Navigate

4
MALL
Oh, no! It's Maria's birthday today. Is there a mall near here?
There's a mall across from the movie theater on Second Avenue.
WHOOSH
5
MALL
TELEPHONE
Thanks, Captain Navigate!
Excuse me. Where's the bus station?
Oh, dear.
Go straight. Take a left. It's next to the library.
BUS STATION
6
7
Don't worry. Don't be late! I'm Captain Navigate.
ZOOM
8
BUS STATION
Thank you.
You're welcome.

Don't worry. Don't be late! I'm Captain Navigate. Ha, ha, ha.
PARK
9
Excuse me. Where's the park?
I'm sorry. I don't know.
Oh, no. I'm late.
PARK
10
11
ALERT
museum
Everybody is lost today! Come on, Sniffer.

12
Look. It's The Loser. He's a bad man.
SWIMMING POOL
13
Ha, ha, ha. This is fun. Hmm ... I'm hungry. Is there a café near here?
SWIMMING POOL
14
Sniffer! Quick! Let's change the sign.
Cafe
15
Oh, no!
Ha, ha, ha. Now, this is fun.

Chapter 6

The Giant Turnip

6
Nadia, where's your mom?
She's in the kitchen. Mom, can you help, please?
7
This is my mom. She's tall and strong.
8
Can I help?
Here's my grandpa.
9
I'm here, too!
And my grandma ... and my dog ... and my cat ... and my cow!
10
Sit down, Grandma. Nadia! Don't play – help!

11
Mooooo!
12
Ooof!
13
HOORAY!
Look. A beautiful, big turnip for the family.
Thank you, everybody!
14
Mmm, turnip soup every day! Let's eat.
Hooray!

Good Friends
Chapter 7
1
Look. It's little Jake, he doesn't have any friends. Ha, ha, ha!
Go away Billy.
2
Doo Da Doo Da Do Da.
What's that?
UFO
3
Doodle.
Hello, there! What's your name?
4
OK Doodle, come with me. Where's your mom? Do you have a mom?
Mama! Mama!
No. I'm not your mom. My name's Jake.
Jakejakejake.
5
Ha, ha! Look, boys. Jake has a new pet. What is it?
I don't know.

6
Eww! It's small and green. Look. It has long arms and short legs.
Ha, ha, ha! Jake has a funny pet. It's ugly.
Ouch! My hand hurts.
7
Come on Doodle. Let's go.
The next day...
8
Mama, Mama!
9
Come back here!
Doodle! Don't go!
10
Mama! Mama!
Help!

11
12
Doodle. Where are you? And where's Billy?
Ha, ha, ha! What is it? It's pink. It's ugly. It has short arms.
Stop! Take me home!
13
14
Ouch! My arm hurts.
Stop! He's my friend.

Jake, Jake, Jake!
15
Friend, friend, friend!
Hello, my little friend.
16
Later ...
17
Goodbye friends!
Goodbye, Doodle!
Thank you, Jake. You're a good friend.

I LIKE CAKE!

Chapter 8

It's Wednesday.
It's lunchtime.
"Is there any cake?"
asks Chip.
7
"No, there isn't," says Chef. "Lunch
today is burgers and peas."
8
"Hmm. Burger, please," says Chip.
"I like burgers, but I don't like peas.
I don't like anything green."
9
It's Thursday. It's lunchtime.
"Is there any cake?" asks
Chip.
10
11
"No, there isn't," says Chef.
"Lunch today is pasta and
broccoli."
"Hmm. Pasta, please,"
says Chip. "I like pasta,
but I don't like broccoli. I
don't like anything green."
12

It's Friday. It's lunchtime. Friday is a special day. Chef has a big cake. "Is there any cake?" asks Chip.
13

"Yes, there is," says Chef. "Do you like cake?"
"Oh, yes, I do!" says Chip.
14

15
"BUT YOU DON'T LIKE ANYTHING GREEN!" says Chef. "Ha, ha, ha!"

Chapter 9

The Magic Violin

1 In our town,
There's a man named Tim.
He can't drive a cart,
But he can play the violin.

2 He can sing and dance,
This man named Tim,
And strange things happen,
When he plays his violin.

3 Look at those fish.
Those fish can fly!

4 Fish can't fly.
Don't be silly, Tim.

5
Oh, yes, they can,
When I play my violin.
6
Look at those birds.
Those birds can dance.
7
Birds can't dance.
Don't be silly, Tim.
8
Oh, yes, they can,
When I play my violin.

9
Look at those cows.
They can climb trees.
10
Cows can't climb trees.
Don't be silly, Tim.
11
Oh, yes, they can,
When I play my violin.
12
Listen to those sheep.
Those sheep can sing!
13
Sheep can't sing.
Don't be silly, Tim.

14
Oh, yes, they can,
When I play my violin.
15
Look at those dogs.
They can skate!
16
Dogs can skate!
You're right, Tim.
17
They can skate,
When you play your violin.
18
In our town,
There's a man named Tim.
Strange things happen,
When he plays his violin.

Macmillan Education Limited
4 Crinan Street
London N1 9XW

Companies and representatives throughout the world

Story Central Plus Level 1 Reader ISBN 978-1-380-06087-7
Story Central Plus Level 1 Reader eBook ISBN 978-1-380-07115-6
Story Central Plus Level 1 Student Book with Reader, Student eBook, Reader eBook, and CLIL eBook ISBN: 978-1-380-06083-9
Story Central Plus Level 1 Student Book with Reader, CLIL Book, Student eBook, Reader eBook, and CLIL eBook ISBN: 978-1-380-06082-2

Written by Viv Lambert ELT Limited and Mo Choy Design Ltd

This edition published 2021
First edition entitled "Story Central" published 2015 by Macmillan Education Limited

Page design, layout and art editing by Wild Apple Design Ltd
Chen's Magic Pen illustrated by Patricia Yuste (Advocate Art); The Princess and the Teddy Bear illustrated by Louise Redshaw (Plum Pudding Illustration); The Hungry Giraffe illustrated by Inna Chernyak (Plum Pudding Illustration); The Mystery House illustrated by Ayesha Lopez (Advocate Art); Captain Navigate illustrated by Stephen Reed (The July Group); The Giant Turnip illustrated by Ellie Jenkins (Advocate Art); Good Friends illustrated by Robin Boyden (Pickled Ink); I Like Cake! illustrated by Marcus Cutler (Sylvie Poggio Artist Agency); The Magic Violin illustrated by Valentina Belloni (MB Artists).

Cover design by Wild Apple Design Ltd
Cover artwork: front cover, Patricia Yuste (Advocate Art), Inna Chernyak (Plum Pudding Illustration), and Stephen Reed (The July Group); back cover, Valentina Belloni (MB Artists) and Marcus Cutler (Sylvie Poggio Artist Agency).

Authors' acknowledgements
Thank you to everyone at Macmillan for their support and for allowing us to work in 'our way'. For patience and tolerance of late-night working, thank you to our families.

Printed and bound in Brazil.
2025
10